Beyond the Literary-Industrial Complex:

> ## How Authors and Publishers Are Using the Amazon Kindle and Other New Technologies to Unleash a 21st-Century Indie Movement of Readers and Writers

By Stephen Windwalker

Author of the bestselling series of articles about the Amazon Kindle

About the Author

Stephen Windwalker writes the indieKindle blog and is the author of several books and numerous short-form pieces of fiction and nonfiction, some under his real name. He has worked as a community organizer, fruit picker, bean counter, sports writer, dishwasher, publishing industry executive, elected official, sandwich maker, and bookseller, among other things.

Windwalker attended and eventually graduated from Harvard College with the help of a full scholarship. While an undergraduate he served as fiction editor of the Harvard Advocate and studied with Monroe Engel, Kurt Vonnegut Jr., Robert Lowell, and Carter Wilson. He lives near Boston and is astonished by the fact that he is the author of the #1 bestselling title in the Amazon Kindle store.

THE BOOK THAT IS HELPING THOUSANDS OF AUTHORS TO UNLEASH A 21ST CENTURY INDIE MOVEMENT OF WRITERS AND READERS...

...by Stephen Windwalker, the man who has learned from his experiences as an author, bookseller, and publishing executive to sell more copies than any other author in Amazon's Kindle Bookstore.

The independent publishing movement includes thousands of writers who toil hard to produce work of distinction and take an entrepreneurial approach to polishing, printing, packaging, marketing and distributing their books themselves.

Our movement also includes many other authors whose work is published by small presses, publishing collectives, and the publishers who constitute the membership of independent publishing organizations like PMA, SPAN, and regional groups or are disciples of self-publishing trailblazers like Dan Poynter.

If you are a serious writer, at any stage of a writing life that involves discipline and daily work and the aspiration, whether realized yet or not, to connect with readers, I intend this book for you.

My purpose here is not to move "beyond books" or to replace them with blogs or e-books or any other medium. Books are sacred things to me, and I would have it that way, with whatever stubbornness I need to muster, always.

Instead, my aim here is to help serious writers use a relatively new set of opportunities to continue and even to enrich their work as writers in ways that are radically different from, yet entirely consistent with, the ways in which writers have been working for centuries. Along the way, it is my hope that the approaches discussed here will help you to get your work into the hands of increasing numbers of readers, and perhaps improve your capacity to earn a decent living from your writing work.

Beyond the Literary-Industrial Complex:

How Authors and Publishers Are Using the Amazon Kindle and Other New Technologies to Unleash a 21st-Century Indie Movement of Readers and Writers

By Stephen Windwalker

Harvard Perspectives Press
hppress@gmail.com
Arlington, Massachusetts
indiekindle.blogspot.com

Beyond the Literary-Industrial Complex: How Authors and Publishers Are Using the Amazon Kindle and Other New Technologies to Unleash an Indie Movement of Readers and Writers By Stephen Windwalker. Copyright 2008, Stephen Windwalker and Harvard Perspectives Press.

Unattributed quotations are by Stephen Windwalker.
ISBN-10   0-9715778-9-7
ISBN-13   978-0-9715778-9-3

First Edition, 2008; First Printing, 2008

CONTENTS

PREFACE

I do not presume to know exactly what brings you here, and so I hope you will forgive me if I do not offer you a specific and rigidly ordered pathway through this book. The velocity of change in our culture -- of the written word, specifically, but also of the arts and the exchange of information generally -- seems to me to require that I try to balance polemic and primer here as I approach my subject. This is not an easy balance to achieve. While there will be highly proficient, inquisitive, polymath readers who will be able to take up this book and manage to navigate in linear fashion from beginning to end as if it had the plot or the spine of a novel or a biography, that is not what I would do. It is not the way I have written the book, and it is not how I would read it if it had arrived in the mail or over the Whispernet from Amazon today.

I also understand, and will not be offended, if you go first to the "how-to" chapters of this book located primarily in Part II. There is plenty of good, nuts-and-bolts information there, and it will serve you well. But I also encourage you to make a point of reading the rest of this book when the time is right, because understanding and engaging your role in the fast-changing world of publishing, and accepting your opportunity to join in building a new indie movement of readers and writers will serve you even better. If you are a writer, it will help you break free from shackles that may be holding you back in your work and to find a zone in which you are a better writer, a more successful author, and an active participant in a vital and important community. If you are a reader, it will help you to connect with a revolutionary indie culture that is expanding our choices, as readers and as humans, on a daily basis.

Because I am aware that many readers will focus surgically on the "primer" chapters that apply specifically to their own publishing needs and interests, I am going to err on the side of being a little redundant in some of the primer chapters with respect to specific instructions. So if you read the chapter on magazine publishing right after you read the first chapter on publishing material for the Kindle, you may experience a bit of a déjà vu feeling with a sentence here or there. The bottom line is that I would rather risk saying something twice than failing to say something that is essential in the place where you expect to find it.

*   *   *

Among all the demons that writers must face down or otherwise make some settlement with, there are perhaps none more banal, insidious, and taxing than those we must challenge or accommodate when we try to work out some way of dealing with the "writer development" industry. It is large, serious, full of seduction and admonition, peopled with venerable mentors and mercenary pretenders, all arranged invitingly where we may have the greatest difficulty discerning between those who can assist us in the complicated processes of connecting our work with readers, of polishing and publishing, of discerning quality and disposing of dreck, and those whose only interest is in depositing our checks or online payments. One need only peruse the ads arrayed in the various writers' trade and craft magazines to conclude that writers spend tens of millions of dollars fueling the writer development industry – on workshops, conferences, retreats, MFA programs, book coaches, writing books, writing software, literary services, magazines, writing contests, vanity presses, advertising, fee-based literary agencies, marketing, and other permutations – all in hopes of taking their work to the next level, and perhaps even of hitting some imagined "big time" as authors.

Some of this money is very well spent. Some of it, whether or not it is well spent in terms of bringing positive results for those spending it, has the palpable benefit of providing support or even a living for serious writers who are themselves employed in this industry in one way or another. Some of it, it will come as no shock when disclose it here, includes the money that writers spend on this book. I make no apology for this fact, but I certainly accept and own the responsibility to do all that I can to make the entire project worth your while and your expenditure.

In this effort to provide something worthy of your time and expense, it is not so much to hedge my bets as to accommodate my passions and my sense of what is most urgent for writers and readers today, that I seek to crowbar what could be three projects into a single book: a primer on the use of new technologies for authors, a clear-eyed look at what the publishing industry has to offer to readers and writers today and how things came to this point, and a polemical call for writers, readers, and others in the book trades to restructure our relationships.

Against the backdrop of this impressive industry, it only makes sense to urge writers to devote a small but significant amount of the time and money, that they might otherwise invest in the writer development industry, to an effort to take some control over their writing careers.

For most of us, I believe, we make our best efforts to take this kind of control when we work to build, to unleash, and to take our places in an indie movement of writers and readers.

It is time to begin.

PART ONE:

THE DREAM
OF CREATIVE INDEPENDENCE

Chapter I.1

The Romance of Submission

What is it to be a writer hard at the work of creating something wonderful, a work in progress that you will chisel away at and breathe life into and perfect until it is published and embraced by a welcoming audience of serious readers who buzz to one another and back to you that you have made something new, something of value, perhaps even something eternal?

In the middle of this faithful process, as you gird yourself against distractions and slave away at MacDowell or Yaddo or Starbucks, or in your garret, or on the Acela, or in your prison cell, there are blissfully intense moments when there is only you and the work. On these days the work is the best of companions.

Such moments may seem to validate Miss Dickinson's pronouncement that "Publication is not the proper business of a poet," so that you are inclined to apply it to your particular form of literary creation, whether it is your *Dream Songs* or your *Ulysses*, your biography of a racehorse, or your treatise on how to solve Sudoku.

But if you are budgeting time and funds so that you can afford enough daycare to allow you to finish your book, or trying to balance your writing with a day job, or to set enough aside to allow you to escape the day job, it may be difficult to fend off those thoughts of publication. If so, as the Belle of Amherst surely knew, these largely economic conditions may carry some strange elemental power – the power, perhaps, of the wolf at your door? – that puts you at risk of losing the very frame of mind that allows you to create something worthwhile in the first place.

I don't wish to provoke hand-wringing, hair-tearing angst or to send ten thousand writers running for fee-based therapeutic relationships that they can ill afford. (Shrinks, in my experience, aren't much good at solving underlying economic problems anyway). There are plenty of activities on the spectrum of creative endeavor where one need not be tied up in knots about one's literary output and its ultimate place in the world. The conventionally established professional author, whose work reaps nice advances and then sells well enough to "earn out" those advances, is usually well enough inoculated against such dreary and careerist considerations that she needs only to balance her writing efforts with such concessions as she may choose to make to her publisher's marketing demands or to the claims of celebrity. Such an author may be the fortunate inhabitant of a "zone" where one is so well guaranteed audience, promotion, distribution, and compensation that such considerations may be treated as trivial afterthoughts. And while some of the habitués of this zone may indeed be hacks who license their characters or record half a dozen formulaic page-turners each year with the next-generation iteration of the Dictaphone, there are others who have worked long and hard at good and durable work that extends our literary culture, fills our leisure hours with civilized delight, and illuminates the human experience.

No doubt there are many other writers of distinction who, keeping closer to Miss Dickinson's dictum, work well and steadily with no regard whatsoever for the business of publication, whether they write only to be writing, for no audience at all, only for themselves, or only against some future time when they will brook their first considerations about what to do with what they have been writing. Perhaps they can work this way because they are the otherwise idle rich, or they combine a good day job with abundant energy and discipline in lives where distractions are scarce, or they are incarcerated or otherwise institutionalized, or they are prohibited for one reason or another from telling their story. But for the vast majority of us who would seek out a place for writing as part or all of the work of our daily lives, neither of these extremes is the reality.

Very few of us are driven by a serious desire to become millionaire authors, but we would like an honest chance to make a decent living writing good books and getting them into the hands of discerning readers. Yet it is in staking even such modest claims for our creative work that we risk subjecting ourselves to a writer's purgatory.

Want to submit your manuscript through traditional publishing channels? Then those "blissfully intense hours when there is only you and the work" are about to be subjected, like a teenager's love affair or even the bonds of best friends or blood brothers, to the intrusive, perverse, distorting pressures of societal judgment. You've been working privately, passionately, one-on-one with your manuscript, teasing and massaging it into the book you have lived to write, but now you must submit it and then wait passively to see if this relationship passes muster in the eyes of agents, editors, publishers, reviewers, and peers. You have quietly bestowed your passion on this companion, and now you must dress it up and take it to the prom. Even if you have always kept your own creative counsel, lived and worked by your own aesthetic, and been your own toughest editor and creative jury, now, by the simple act of inviting your companion into the glare of public scrutiny, as if assuming fairness in its consideration, you are turning the tables on yourself.

By accepting your role in this aptly named submission process, you are implicitly validating its legitimacy and encouraging its cliques of rather mean-spirited girls and boys. Later, as you open and file away their rejection slips, you will of course be formalizing and finalizing the concomitant process of obliterating your own confidence in your capacity to create, to evaluate, to rethink, and to revise what you are creating. As in most initially blissful high school romances, once they are subjected to the harsh judgments of the reigning popular crowd, someone is bound to get dumped.

It isn't hard to imagine the famous final scene of break-up dialogue between a fickle novelist and his manuscript – what, your fiction doesn't talk back to you? – as the pages are about to be consigned to the back of the file cabinet or the hard drive's least trafficked subdirectory….

"Shit! I thought you loved me. All you wanted was to get published!"

"Well, sure. After I spent every day with you for two years, it would have been nice."

"I never realized that was the only reason you were interested in me."

"Oh, c'mon. Don't guilt trip me. Can't you accept that I have needs too?"

"If that's all you were looking for, why didn't you just pay for it?"

"Pay for it?"

"Sure. Why not? There are plenty of places where you could take your money and your so-called needs and get published without—"

"Without what?"

[Tears]

"Without paying any attention to what's really inside me."

"Maybe. I mean, I suppose. But I would never want it to get around that I was paying for it."

"It's hard to believe that you're the same one who believed in me."

"Oh, come on. Was I supposed to totally ignore the things that Lindsay and Winona and Heather were saying about you?"

"Hah! They call themselves agents and editors. They are nothing more than glorified slush-pile interns."

"Well, everybody else listens to them. I'm never going to make it as a published author if I don't listen to what they say. I know they will want to publish me if I can just go back to the drawing board and tighten up the story line a little."

"Story line? What about my characters?"

"It was nice, baby. You know I will never forget you. Maybe if I can just get published we can get together sometime, in the future."

Okay, this bit of fun has its limits, but hopefully it has helped to illuminate a worthwhile distinction: too often, it would be more apt to mangle Miss Dickinson's phrases by noting that it is not publication, but submission, that is not the proper business of poets and other writers.

Is there a choice?

We have ceded to the major publishing houses and their gatekeepers the central roles in determining which written creative work will be widely disseminated in our culture, and in the process we subject ourselves as writers, and to a lesser but still significant degree as readers, to agonies of waiting, wishing and hoping, and quiet desperation. It was not gratuitously that publishers established this hegemony, with its concomitant power over our creative and intellectual lives. There was, especially in the half-century between 1920 and 1970, a golden age of American publishing. Many of the subsidiary "imprints" of today's global media empires were, then, small, fairly informal shops where editors were motivated by their passion for literature, where an author celebrating the publication of his novel or not quite making it to his next royalty check or advance might well be found, of a morning, sleeping one off on the sofa in one of his editor's homey book-lined offices. Almost everything about the book industry, from the ubiquitous independent bookshops to the number of books reviewed or excerpted in mass-circulation magazines like the *Saturday Evening Post* or *Collier's*, to the abundance of serious "mid-list" titles kept in print by publishers, was well laid out for a mass culture of readers, and thus, in turn, for the care and feeding of enough quality writers to keep the culture in good books.

Lest I seem to be invoking some nostalgic "It's Morning Again in America" sepia tone of a glorious past, I recommend Jason Epstein's thoughtful and intelligent 2001 memoir of that era in the history of the publishing industry, *Book Business: Publishing Past Present and Future*. Of course there were market forces, personal ambitions, and intra- and inter-corporate competition at work in the publishing industry between 1920 and 1970, and barriers organized around class pedigree, racism, and sexism were every bit as prevalent in the publishing industry as they were in American society at large. But the fact remains that before the dramatic, power-concentrating frenzy of mergers and acquisitions that occurred in the last third of the century, the American publishing industry was generally keeping up its end of the bargain with the country's creative culture and its audience of readers.

Writers submitted their work to agents and editors with some faith that it would get a reading, and thus would be given all the chance that any writer could expect. There was an ample array of potential entry markets, including college and literary magazines, the pulps, and even a surprising number of slick mass-market magazines that gave significant space to fiction each month and paid competitively for it. Mass periodicals from the *Saturday Evening Post* to *Time*, whatever their politics might be, were self-conscious of a responsibility to guide and broaden the culture, if perhaps not to deepen it, rather than merely to reflect its shortcomings.

In other words, there was a long period in American publishing when one could observe significant correspondence between the best work that was being written by our novelists and poets and biographers and the work that the "popular crowd" of publishing gatekeepers was admitting into its world of published books. During most of this time, our Anglo-American culture did much to promote its own better moments: Epstein notes that authors from James Joyce to James Baldwin used to grace the covers of *Time* magazine. Today, in a kind of weird apotheosis of the real and metaphorical linkages between high school clique culture and American literary culture, the bestselling author you are most likely to see on magazine covers at your favorite newsstand may well be Paris Hilton.

The reasons why Ms. Hilton is a bestselling author are perhaps more interesting than most of what one will find between the covers of her books. Publishing houses search out brand-name celebrities whose platforms guarantee bestseller status, because both the publishing houses and the retail bookstore chains desperately need high turnover bestsellers to generate the revenue necessary to justify their existence in a world of literary-industrial conglomerates that is, increasingly, all about the bottom line. Such name-brand authors may be genre fiction writers who have identified a certain formula for repetitive mass-market success and are willing to abide by their publishers' pleas not to monkey with the formulas. But just as often these days the celebrity authors are cross-over stars: people who are cashing in on the notoriety they've gained on MTV, Court TV, *American Idol*, ESPN, *Entertainment Tonight*, *People*, their own television or radio shows, or, given its increasing "news" coverage of the icons who become known to us through these aforementioned portals of mass culture, the network news.

It shouldn't shock us that readers buy a lot of these mass-produced cookie-cutter books. First, they are only one more confirming symptom of the national multi-media fixations that have already been proven for OJ, Wacko Jacko, Britney, Paris, Monica, and so forth. Second, sometimes there is interesting material in these books. Finally, although the range of more interesting alternatives to such books is definitely not narrowing, our public access to them is limited because neither the publishers, the chain bookstores, or the big-box stores whose deeply-discounted offerings of a few hundred bestsellers often drive independent booksellers out of business are willing to make a marketing or space-allocation commitment to books that do not stack up, from the get-go, as bestsellers. If you are looking for something to read on your flight, there are only so many titles available at the airport bookstand, and all of them are there because the corporate buyers or distributors are certain that they will be bestsellers and that "you" are most likely to buy a book by an author you've heard about already.

New York Times columnist David Brooks, in a Spring 2008 piece on niche political marketing, drew a clear portrayal of the largely homogeneous culture that existed in America before anyone had ever heard of niche markets and long-tail economics:

"Fifty-five years ago, 80 percent of American television viewers, young and old, tuned in to see Milton Berle on Tuesday nights. Tens of millions, rich and poor, worked together at Elks Lodges and Rotary Clubs. Millions more, rural and urban, read general-interest magazines like *Look* and *Life*. In those days, the owner of the local bank lived in the same town as the grocery clerk, and their boys might play on the same basketball team. Only 7 percent of adult Americans had a college degree."

Entering the book section of a Walmart or BJ's has something in common with stepping into the 1950s in terms of the diversity of culture and selection. If you have written one of the top 500 novels of the year, but it never makes it into the top 300, it is unlikely that it will turn up on the bookshelves in those short-tail book departments. None of this is great news for readers, but it can be especially depressing for serious writers, because the big cultural picture distills to a very simple message: the mainstream publishing industry, to the extent that it is embodied in the five global media empires that dominate the American book trade at this writing, is not interested in what you are writing, is not going to make meaningful judgments about your work based on the quality or distinctiveness of your content, and is instead much more interested in hooking up with someone who is already "popular," even if it means hiring someone else (you, perhaps?) to do the ghost writing. The industry's popular-crowd cliques, it turns out, are not fair, and they could care less about what you may think is special about your "companion" of the last couple of years.

Chapter I.2

Outside Your Control:
Submitting a Manuscript
Via the Traditional Publishing Route

Let's imagine for starters that you are a first-time, unknown author, and you have just finished the process of writing and polishing of a damned good manuscript. Fiction, nonfiction, memoir, how-to, it could be any of these, but the point is, it's good. It's a book that will make a difference in people's lives. Not only do you know this -- passionately and proudly, we might add – but others whose judgment and objectivity you trust have read your manuscript and given you an honest but very positive appraisal. This is especially meaningful after you have paid attention to their sometimes difficult-to-hear constructive criticism in the early going.

First, congratulations. Celebrate your achievement. There are tens of millions of people who fancy that they have a book in them, but you are one of the few who kept your focus, did the work, completed the marathon, delivered the baby.

So, what's next? *There's more? I can't just sell the film rights and move into the trophy house? You mean I have to raise the kid too? You mean I completed the marathon only to find out that it's one of those Ironman Triathlon deals, and now I have miles of cycling and swimming to go before I sleep?*

Possibly so. It's your call, but let's take a look at your options.

With a bow to the Book Industry Statistics page on Dan Poynter's publishing website at http://bookstatistics.com, let's start by considering a few numbers related to your chances for success if you follow the traditional publishing route.

Step 1

Your first step, once your manuscript is ready to go, will be to send it off to agents and/or editors. You'll buy or borrow an up-to-date directory of writer's markets, select one or more initial destinations, and put to work your years of reading articles and perhaps even books about how to submit a manuscript, how to query and approach the agents and editors who are powerful gatekeepers at this stage of the game, how to write a snappy but professional cover letter, and so forth. But you are happy to do this drudge work, to step ever so lightly on its attendant eggshells, to don an attitude of submission, because you are confident it is but a brief passage, rich in dramatic irony.

Once the first agent opens your package (Fed Ex or at least Priority Mail or UPS Blue, of course, to make it stand out!) and begins to read, all will be right in the world. You'll be swept off to Manhattan for lunches and manuscript auctions and you and the agent and your manuscript will immediately be bathed in the warm glow of your imminent success and fame.

Bzzzzzzz. Yes, that's the Wrong Answer Buzzer.

The reality is that about one in every 6,000 unsolicited manuscripts gets so much as a reading from an editor or agent with decision-making authority. Even gets read. What's black and white but almost never read? Yep, your manuscript. If you are already some kind of star, or if you have your own platform with significant exposure to a specific swath of the reading public, great. Otherwise, whether or not your manuscript gets read has nothing to do with its quality. It is, to use a phrase you will want to remember, outside your control.

Step 2

But let's say you hit the lottery and work every flimsy connection you can dream up and your manuscript gets read. Now your chances for success have improved dramatically. You've made it into what is very bluntly referred to as the "slush pile." What, now, are the odds against a mainstream publisher actually deciding to offer you a publishing contract? Somewhere between 50 to 1 and 1,000 to 1, depending on the credibility and tenacity of your agent (if you have one) and initial reader, on the internal financial pressures facing your prospective publishers, on the degree of verticality in their decision-making structures, and, to a possibly lesser extent, on the quality of your submission. If any of the individuals assigned to vet your "project" can't muster passionate feelings for it, it will probably be rejected. You've also entered an area here where the quality of your manuscript may work against you if it raises the reading bar too high for some imagined common denominator of readers, so the bottom line here is that, especially when compounded with the odds against you for Step 1, your chances of achieving a positive outcome now in Step 2 are....

What are they?

Yes. Outside your control.

New York Times Book Review editor Rachel Donadio, in a June 26, 2005 penultimate-page essay, described with acerbic accuracy the other factors that weigh just as heavily as literary quality in the kinds of judgments that publishers bring to bear on what they will publish or promote, and that bookstore buyers factor into their decisions on how many copies they order and, just as important, what kind of placement to give those copies in their stores:

"How promotable is the author? Can the author appear in public without freaking out? Will the author do well on television? Does the author have a platform – a built-in audience around a specific theme?"

Where such preoccupations ultimately lead, Donadio says, is to the quest for the attractive, telegenic author, and "jacket photos of writers looking as sexy as possible, be they men a la mode de Sebastian Junger, adventure journalist extraordinaire, or brainy men looking sultry, or brainy women showing lots of skin."

No wonder Walt Whitman, James Joyce, and Allen Ginsberg decided to start out with indie publishing efforts!

But, you saw, whatever. No problem. You want to monetize your manuscript, to use a bit of business-page jargon? You'll just have to be prepared to spend enough time at the gym to allow a publisher to commoditize you as the book's author.

Step 3

But we begin with the assumption that everyone who has bought *this* book is an attractive person. You are attractive and tenacious and thorough and you've shown just the right balance of audacity, humility, and leg to navigate the minefield up to now. You get a book contract. You sign it, and start wondering what to wear when they ask you to appear on Oprah. But hold on there, just a minute.

The next step, wherein it is determined whether anyone ever hears about your book beyond your high school classmates and your extended family – writing program classmates don't count, because even if they say otherwise they will be pissed off when they see your name in print – concerns your book's chances of getting promoted well by your publisher. Remember the five books that were finalists for the 2004 National Book Award in Fiction? Good literary fiction by "unknown authors," and prior to their nomination there is little evidence that any of them received anything of value from their publishers in the form of promotion. The major book marketing elements in the traditional promotional repertoire of big publishers -- author tours, ads in the major literary, trade, consumer, and bibliophile periodicals, co-op advertising budgets for booksellers, and even bookstore placement fees -- all require significant money and some adult continuity of attention from serious, credible marketing people. If a book reviewer or review assignment editor does not see the existence of such support, the book is unlikely to get a review regardless of its quality. This is not snobbery or snarkiness; it is a simple matter of overwhelming arithmetic.

According to R.R. Bowker there were 291,920 new book titles published in 2006, and it has been estimated that publishers send out about 20 million advance reading copies each year to review media, bookstore and distributor buyers, and opinion leaders. A very small percentage of these new titles get read by reviewers, or ordered and stocked by physical bookstores. Publishers are notorious for failing to back up the initial promotional campaign commitments they make to debut authors, and also for such high attrition and staff-shuffling rates that the editors and marketing types who were around when you signed your book contract are often long gone at the time of your book's publication. The new crew knows nothing about the handshake commitments that were made to you or your agent then, and frankly, please don't take this the wrong way, but they are a little perplexed that the decision to publish your book was made in the first place.

So. All we are really trying to say here is that this question of whether your book is well promoted is, well, out of your control.

Have I painted too bleak a picture? Possibly – but what I have said here is based on years of experience in the book trades, as a publishing executive in one of the big five global publishing empires, and as bookseller, reviewer, author, and independent publisher. The specific numbers may involve some estimates and may fluctuate from year to year, but they are close enough to accurate that you should take the fundamental point, and the forces I have described are the real forces that move decisions with traditional publishers. If you want to go that route, be my guest. But be aware that, in order to have even the outside chance for success that I have tried to describe above, you will have to invest months, and possibly even years, in the process.

Perhaps it is time to consider another route.

*   *   *

It doesn't have to be this way. A large part of the problem is that the "traditional" relationships between writers, agents, and publishers have become so perverse and dysfunctional that writers form understandably diabolical expectations about what may be required even to get a fair reading for their work, and consequently in many cases they may censor rather than polish their own work, and pervert their talents, in a seldom successful attempt to accommodate the gatekeepers of the publishing industry.

Although I fully accept and embrace the need for writers to comport themselves professionally and present their work appropriately in their approaches to agents and editors, I have grown weary of reading comments by agents saying how they have no choice but to return manuscripts if, say, they find a typo in the first five pages. (Think I'm exaggerating? Check almost any issue of *Writer's Digest*.) While it is true that writers ought to be able to submit more polished packages now in the era of Spell-Check programs and word processing, agents and editors would not be quite so insufferable if they didn't cast themselves as the types of people who would be eager to stamp "RETURN TO SENDER" on a submission from Hemingway or Harper Lee if a word was misspelled or an agent's name typed incorrectly.

So, before we embark on our road map of what it takes to achieve independent publishing success, let's observe some things that you will not have to do to be successful:

· You will not have to walk on eggshells with agents and editors, because your decision to publish can be your own, backed up by your own significant investment of time and, perhaps, of money.

· You will not have to give yourself a skull-splitting headache trying to reduce your Great American Novel or well-researched, elegantly written nonfiction book into a 30-second "elevator pitch" in the hope that you will bump into an agent at your cousin's wedding or have a chance encounter with Stephen King at Fenway and find him more interested in helping you get published than in the name of the kid lefty the Sox are bringing in from the pen.

Chapter I.3

The Rise of Indie Movements

If you are reading this book, there is a very good chance that, consciously or not, you are (or soon will be) part of a revolutionary movement that has already begun to transform the world of writing and publishing and reading.

Perhaps you are already aware of your participation in this tide of change. Or perhaps you are thinking about these issues for the first time.

So, what does it mean to be part of the independent publishing movement?

Is it just a fancy or circuitous way of saying that a writer is self-published?

Certainly not. Many self-published authors are part of this movement, but not all. Somebody who lays out thousands of dollars to a vanity publisher for the temporary ego boost of having printed copies of his novel or memoir is, frankly, just a patsy for the publisher's profitable scheme, even if he doesn't realize it until he notices that he still has a basement or garage full of books five years later. There is nothing "independent" at all in that process.

While it is just as difficult to come up with a rigid definition for "indie writer" or "indie publisher" as it has been for "indie musician" or "indie filmmaker," the fact is that in recent years it has increasingly been in the "indie" movement of each of these art forms that the most interesting, distinguished and provocative work has been produced.

In the world of filmmaking, the Nominating Committee of the Independent Spirit Awards applies reasonable guidelines -- uniqueness of vision; original, provocative subject matter; economy of means; and percentage of financing from independent sources – but there's plenty of controversy nonetheless. To the extent that "indie" becomes a badge of positive branding distinction, the controversy begins to heat up.

In the world of book publishing, coming up with a suitable taxonomy to judge what is truly "indie" is not made less challenging by the need to define out the negative branding distinction of vanity publishing and the more amateurish extremes of self-publishing. It would be pretty if we could confer special positive branding distinction with the word "indie," as a kind of shorthand by which potential readers could anticipate a work's quality as distinguished from so much of the dreck turned out by publishers whose primary litmus test for publication often seems to revolve around the questions of whether an author has an existing television, radio or internet porn platform or the proven status associated with prior bestsellers. But it is never that simple.

As actress Laura Linney said in a recent interview when asked to compare her work in indie vs. commercial films: "There are as many bad independent films as there are bad commercial films. I've been in some very good commercial films." In order for people – as audience – to determine what they like, someone has to see the movies, and someone has to read the books. Which is, of course, exactly the way it should be.

The book trades are going through dramatic changes that will affect readers and authors and all of the people who play any role in the process of bring words into "print" and connecting them with readers. Technologies such as the Kindle and Amazon's CreateSpace print-on-demand platform will be at the center of many of these changes, and this book will focus both on how to make the most of these changes in your own career as a writer and on the importance of these changes to our future literary well-being. It is no easy task to dress a how-to book as a manifesto, or a manifesto as a how-to book, but my goal here is to provide a substantial contribution in each category.

With the coming of the Amazon Kindle and CreateSpace, it is fair to say that it has never been easier for writers to publish their writing and make it available to readers. That is the good news, and it may also be the bad news.

Precisely because it is now so easy to "jump" these hurdles that are effectively resting at ground level and thus to meet this minimum definition of what it is to be a published author, there will be problems.

There will be more bad, mediocre, or simply sloppy writing published than ever before. There's not a lot that can be done about this. Just a year ago the price of entry to self-publish a short print run of a book, say 3,000 copies, was several thousand dollars. Print-on-demand packages came with significant set-up fees, costly incremental per-unit charges, and weak marketing and distribution linkages. Now, it doesn't cost a dime to publish a Kindle edition, and Amazon's CreateSpace subsidiary makes print-on-demand free as well, while also tying it seamlessly to powerful distribution channels. I don't mean to imply any connection between writing talent and the ability to cough up a few thousand bucks, but it's possible that in the past that price of entry might have inspired some would-be authors to spend more time getting feedback and polishing their work before publication.

Even when the writing is good, too many authors will approach the do-it-yourself project of publishing their work as if there was nothing more involved than the writing itself. Since they do not need to think of publication as a business transaction, some may not the serious attention to marketing and presentation that is essential to success.

Perhaps we should be more troubled by this potential proliferation of work of lesser merit, but I'm not. I think I have some pretty good reasons:

· First, no trees will lose their lives in the publication of Kindle editions. Indeed, one of the exciting things about the

Kindle in general is its long-term potential for inspiring more reading while reducing the carbon footprint of reading books and newspapers.

· With respect to Kindle editions, other e-books, and print-on-demand, the number of books "published" will be driven very specifically by the number of buyers or readers they have. Happily, this will reduce clutter and distraction at the same time it saves trees, gasoline, and other resources.

· I guess I'm just not much of a snob. Although I have very clear ideas about what I like and don't like, I usually refuse to impose them on others and I have trouble even bringing myself to write passages like the one above about "bad, mediocre, or simply sloppy writing." If someone spends years of his life writing a book, and he wants to make it available for others to read, he should do that. And, as always, beauty is in the eye of the beholder.

· So, how do we keep from being buried in reading choices? We connect with each other as readers and authors to communicate about what we like, what we value, and what works for us. As authors and publishers, we encourage sampling in much the same way that musicians do, and we take advantage of the ample opportunities that Amazon, and especially the Kindle environment, provides for connecting with readers who are looking for the kind of writing we do, our topics, etc. Over time, I expect that the Kindle will do a lot to strengthen the engagement of readers with each other and with authors as well.

At the risk that I may be rendering into vapor all efforts to come up with a clear definition of the independent publishing movement, let me advance the notion that, on some essential level, participation in this movement amounts to a state of mind. My point is that those of us who take independent publishing seriously understand that the quality of our work and the connections and the community that we are able to build with each other and with our readers are far more important than our capacity to win for our writing the imprimatur of any major publishing house.

This approach to the process of publishing, distributing, and building audience for the written word is not mere rebelliousness. We begin with a clear-eyed assessment of what the major corporate publishers can and cannot do for us. We understand that we are part of long tradition of independently and self-published authors – men and women who understand that their success requires hard work, good writing, and an entrepreneurial approach. We are willing to look past the stigma attached to such work both by the self-serving (and sometimes panic-prone) gatekeepers of the book trade and by people who simply don't understand how things really work in the world of publishing.

We are active agents of change, and consequently it is our business and responsibility to understand and participate in the fast-moving changes that have been taking place during the past two decades, and will continue to take place, in the world of publishing and disseminating the written word. Many of us have been participants in digital short-run publishing efforts, in blogging, in the zine movement, and in e-book publishing long before the advent of the Kindle, Create Space, and their revolutionary publishing platforms. We also recognize as cousins, if not siblings in our indie publishing family, the artists who forged the indie music, indie film, and hip hop movements during the past few decades.

We are possessed, by definition, of an inclusive spirit, and yet we understand, like the practitioners of any other trade, the importance of vigilance against mediocrity and shoddiness and poor workmanship. We believe in and value the possibilities that can occur at the nexus of commerce and culture, yet we have seen with great sadness what has occurred in the corporate publishing industry when commerce is allowed to dominate culture.

We are not doctrinaire ideologues. While we certainly can generate enthusiasm for the notion of taking the tools of literary production into our own hands as writers and readers, we must look for help wherever we can find it in our efforts to build connection and community between readers and writers. When one of us achieves a level of success that causes the big publishers to come calling, it would be juvenile to call that author a sell-out. Instead, we should call her one of our success stories.

Conversely, the more we succeed in building an indie publishing movement and an indie literary movement, the more we can expect efforts to emulate and co-opt these movements. We shouldn't be surprised to find publishers that put one hand out to seek the branding cachet of the indie movement even as they continue, with the other hand, to publish the literary scribbling of Paris Hilton, O.J. Simpson and Ann Coulter.

The grand old keepers of the book trade, from the golden age of the American publishing industry to the favorite bookstores of our youth, are long gone. The often-chronicled story of the corporate mergers and acquisitions that have fueled these changes is a dull economic history.

We understand that what has occurred in the book trade is not so different from what has occurred in other arts and industries: newspapers, film, music, dance and the stage all come to mind. After decades and decades of watching the big fish eat the small, it is becoming clear that the fastest fish now eat the slow, or simply satisfy themselves on an alternative repast while the slow fish die away.

So it must be our business to move quickly, to see our opportunities and seize them, and to be artful entrepreneurs and entrepreneurial artists where culture and commerce meet.

Because of what we do and our affinity for the independent publishing movement, we will hear and read frequent references to things like the *Self-Publishing Hall of Fame*. It is definitely worth checking out the amazing list on John Kremer's website or buying its paperback version. Indeed, part of how we build this movement is to educate ourselves and others about its traditions and its trailblazers. Our familiarity with this history can help us to remove, for ourselves and others, the stigma that occurs when readers lump all self-publishers together with vanity publishers and spammers.

This may sound like a peculiar suggestion to make to artists who are opting in to a movement defined by its "independence," but I believe that all of us in this movement should make a pointed practice of following, learning from, and often emulating a dozen or so men and women whom I will refer to here as trailblazers of the indie literary movement. Some of them may deserve to be called heroes and heroines, or mentors, or even stars, but we will stop short of such labels here. Some are phenomenally successful and generally more associated with the mega corporate publishers than with independent publishing or self-publishing. Others have been phenomenally successful as self-publishers. But in every case they have been trailblazers, they have exhibited a communitarian and independent spirit in their work and in the ways in which they have related to other authors, to the publishing industry, and to readers, booksellers and others.

I will propose here some nominees for your consideration as trailblazers in independent publishing. In subsequent chapters I will highlight the important contributions that some of them have made to building an indie movement in our literature, but for now I will simply provide a list of suggested nominees. This should be a fluid list to which you should make your own additions and feel free to pass by anyone you judge to be unworthy of the mantle. Originally my plan was to provide a tidy little bio box on each, but I realized that such helpfulness, while well-intention, would be counter to my own purposes here. Conducting your own research and bookmarking web pages where you will be able to learn more is part of the process that I am suggesting.

Here are my suggestions: Lawrence Ferlinghetti, Dan Poynter, Vickie Stringer, Stephen King, Jan Nathan, Dave Eggers, Bill James, John Kremer, Ben Franklin, and Christopher Paolini. As you may already be aware, these are men and women who have played a range of different roles in helping to breathe an independent spirit into our literature. Some are indie publishers; some have made important contributions of other kinds. What each of them has shared is an inclusive spirit, a willingness to take risks and to reject conventional categories and norms, and a communitarian approach that has driven them to reach out to others to help expand this movement.

(Now that I have offered this array of indie publishing trailblazers, let me not delay in inserting a pointed disclaimed. While these are venerable people who have done much to bring about the changes that we now see in the indie publishing culture, my selection of them says as much about me – and the fact that I have come through the print-on-paper indie publishing births and rebirths of the past few decades rather than arriving here anew with the dawn of the digital – as it does about them. And so I exhort you to do what we all must do given the velocity of cultural and technical change: keep your eyes on the future, on both the changes and the change makers. Choose your own new generations of trailblazers, and they will not only show you where the future changes will occur. They will just as likely accept you into their tribes, and empower you as you empower yourself to become one of them, a change agent in your own right.)

My purpose in proposing these trailblazers is not to establish a pantheon, but to suggest strongly that we can all learn much by keeping a close eye on what such trailblazers are doing. Check out their websites (and let me know if you find Ben's site or blog!), read what they write, and learn about how they got their start or in some cases about what experiments they tried along the way.

Given the velocity of change in the world of publishing, it behooves any serious author to become an informed participant by becoming a student of its trailblazers, neologisms, and buzzwords and even, perhaps, an early adopter of its gadgets. To put an even finer point on my pitch to you here, I would suggest that anyone who reads this book is dipping only one toe in the water of indie publishing if he fails to read the books by Dan Poynter and John Kremer that I recommend in the bibliography at the end of this volume and to become a subscriber to Dan Poynter's free email newsletter.

Beyond the romance of participating in a movement, the work is relentless. For many independent author-publishers, the operative definition of "independent" is the one that makes it clear that you may be wearing many, and perhaps all, of the hats: writing, editing, formatting, design and creative, marketing, publishing, warehousing, distribution, fulfillment, customer service, paying the bills, receivables and collections, and on and on. Each of these areas of work requires a serious commitment, and if you do not possess the skills, energy and time to meet your responsibilities in any of these areas, or the ability to delegate them to those who do possess such skills, energy and time, there is no point in going forward as an independent publisher.

While writing is usually a solitary process, an ideal approach to much of the work of independent publishing is to build a community or a collective to share what can be shared among its tasks. Obviously and importantly, such community can be beneficial to the essential pre-publication process of getting honest feedback on a manuscript. Equally important, as an indie publishing collective matures it can develop important skill matches for tasks like design, proofreading and editing, while continuing to turn things like mailings that might otherwise be drudgery into more festive social events. A fortuitous additional benefit of such communitarian approaches follows from the fact that other writers are often our best readers. With a bit of encouragement and interactive cooperation, they can also be our best book buyers, reviewers, and blurb writers.

* * *

The energies that give force to independent culture form a strange and unpredictable mix: timid one-to-one conversations can begin to create interest that ultimately may take on the force of a tsunami, seeking out nearly every nook and cranny of potential audience with a new, channel-cutting fierceness of its own. What we have observed with music and film will apply in time to other media as technology explodes and the consumerist tendencies of "early adopters" – those who give the lie to dinosaur caveats such as "Who will ever order books online?"

and "Who will ever download music onto a computer?" and "Who will ever forsake Dan Rather to get their news from bloggers?" – become a culture, ever smaller and crustier, unto themselves.

In an early adopters' culture, technology and content can almost appear to merge as tastemakers distinguish themselves to the point where they are, at once, brand, brander, and branded: witness the rise of podcasters and netcasters such as Santa Monica's KCRW.com, which is building a global online listener base and creating both a national brand and an influential branding agency on the back of its longtime successful weekday program *Morning Becomes Eclectic*, the first U.S. radio program to play Dido, Coldplay, and Norah Jones. KCRW and similar programming like *World Café* (syndicated by Philadelphia's WXPN) and *The Coffee House* (on Boston's WERS) are all leveraging their tastemaker roles to fill the cultural vacuum left in the wake of the vapid, predictable, mind-numbing programming of commercial radio – including, of course, the "revolutionary" stations of a previous generation like Boston's WBCN.

(I don't know if anyone has stated the indie imperative for musicians more eloquently than Tom Petty here: "I couldn't exist nowadays. I could never have built a career like I've had if I were just starting out now. Radio doesn't take a chance on anything anymore; they've streamlined the playlists to the lowest common denominator. It's really kind of silly that they think people would rather hear 'Stairway to Heaven' one more time than a new song.")

Are any of these developments truly significant, or do they all wind themselves into a loopy existential wormhole where we double back to find that Sisyphus keeps pushing his rock, all revolutions become revolting, and Robert Redford announces the opening of chains of theaters to show "indie films" and sell ten-dollar popcorn?

In his visionary 1967 essay, "Towards a Semiological Guerilla Warfare" the novelist Umberto Eco proclaimed that the key to true cultural significance depends on the intense and activist connectedness between audience and artist (or receiver and transmitter):

> "The receiver of the message seems to have a residual freedom: the freedom to read it in a different way…. The battle for the survival of man as a responsible being in the Communications Era is not to be won where the communication originates, but where it arrives…. I am proposing an action to urge the audience to control the message and its multiple possibilities of interpretation…. One medium can be employed to communicate a series of opinions on another medium…. The universe of Technological Communication would then be patrolled by groups of communications guerillas, who would restore a critical dimension to passive reception."

More recently, Naomi Klein has coined the somewhat ponderous phrase "semiotic Robin Hoodism" in urging a vigilant cultural citizenry to take "in-your-face advertising spaces" away from rich corporations and to give them back to the poor. As much as I would love to be able to throw in some language here about controlling the means of production, so as to recover the lost tablets that would enable me to connect all of this with the theories of Marx and Lenin, I will settle for something more general: a call for a communitarian sense of responsibility to each other, as readers and writers, and to our culture of reading and writing, which the secular humanist in me sees, quite often, as our main chance at realizing the sublime in our daily lives.

By heralding and thus extending the life of the good work of others, as readers, writers, and citizens, we are casting bread upon the water. We writers have had to face up to the fact that our initial hopes, that we might happily pursue our writing lives in a Garden of Eden, assured of a loving audience as large as we had any cause to imagine, forgiving of our flaws, where all our needs would be fulfilled, turned out to be delusional. We have been banished to the real world and cursed, like Eve and Adam, to work hard for a living. But it is work that we can do, and be happy to do.

Few if any of us can afford to buy our way into the national consciousness, and there are not enough Oprahs to carry us all on her back(s), but this is where the democratizing power of the internet comes into play: not to democratize literature, but to democratize marketing. The web provides a national buzz network for publishers and authors who cannot afford full-page ads and six-figure marketing budgets. Publishers, authors, and readers will determine for themselves who speaks with authenticity and who brands themselves with work of quality and distinction. In a sense, then, we will elect our own cultural gatekeepers and tastemakers, by voting with our feet, or perhaps with our clicks, and in the voting we will all be gatekeepers of our own domains.

Just as independent films began to steal away box-office from Hollywood blockbusters in the last couple of decades, it is likely that literary, niche-market, and independently published books are positioned to chip away a significant portion of the book audience that has been forsaken by an increasingly concentrated group of major publishers desperate to hit their revenue benchmarks by signing brand-name book contracts with barely literate celebrity authors.

The more dramatic development is the growth of, and the artist's affordable access to distribution channels for, an audience with a demonstrable interest in new and distinctive work. In each field of creative endeavor – film, music, and books – it is the relatively new and simultaneous presence of these several conditions that gives economic and creative traction to an indie movement.

What is independent or "indie"? Independent film and independent music are, among other things, mostly generic, positive labels, like "organically grown" or "low-fat." Since, in the arts, these are not regulated labels, the "indie" designation is subject to intimations, interpretations, and associations that can vary widely from the mind of one prospective audience member to another. It can be tough to pin down whether such a label refers to the producing or manufacturing process, the distribution entity, the genre, the budget, the artistic quality, or the target audience. If a film comes from Fox Searchlight, or is shown on the Independent Film Channel, is it, willy-nilly, an indie film? What if it is screened at the Sundance Film Festival or shown on the Sundance Channel or in the Sundance theater chain? What if it is directed by Robert Redford, or stars him?

* * *

Publishers and booksellers use a variety of organizing devices, including imprints, niche book clubs, publishing company names and reputations, series marketing, titles and subtitles and cover design, and awards, nominations, and blurbs to enable their marketing people, readers, reviewers, and eventually even authors to communicate something meaningful to each other about quality, category or genre, audience, and even something about the brain cell count that a book might require of its readers. If a reader sees a book packaged as a Vintage Contemporary, a Doubleday Anchor, a Penguin Classic or one of City Lights' Pocket Poets series, one can be reasonably sure it is not "mind candy." In some cases such devices even acquire some of the special branding value that an in-the-know audience might associate with the idea of "indie" films or music. In the case of the Vintage Contemporaries series, there was nothing "indie" about the series or the company (Random House) behind it, but a display rack of trade-sized titles by Kay Gibbons, Andre Dubus, Charles Willeford, Joy Williams, and other authors who were not full-fledged bestselling brand names but who, say, were regularly reviewed in The New York Review of Books still, taken together, had the branding power to attract self-identified literary readers in significant numbers by identifying themselves to readers who were hoping to find the next generation of interesting American novelists after Vonnegut, Morrison, and Roth. For Ferlinghetti's City Lights series, he brought together a truly upstart, independent publishing company, the reputation (as well as the access to distribution channels) ofa legendary independent bookstore well-known as a hub and gathering place of the Beats, his own considerable and well-deserved reputation as a poet, and a distinctive, downbeat book design package that nailed the delicate balance between being attractive and recognizable and looking as if it had been produced on a shoestring. More recently, and rather cynically, publishers seem determined to set new records for sameness by producing cover after cover designed to convince juvenile and fantasy readers that they are looking at yet another Harry Potter package.

Let's be honest, authors and future authors.

Our passion for the possibility and potential of an independent publishing movement is informed by a number of high-minded and communitarian ideas, but at its foundation there is something very basic.

We want to publish our work. That is our hope, our ambition, and our plan. Not that there's anything wrong with that. There isn't. There really, really isn't.

We have talent, and we want to put it to the best use possible. We are willing to work hard at this process, to sacrifice, even to keep a day job if we must. But we want readers to read our work. We want to create something of distinction, something that will last, something that will help us to pay the bills. This is good.

Let's talk a bit about what we have had to put up with, as writers. Better yet, I'll talk, and you listen. Perhaps you will find something to identify with in my story.

When I was coming up, the late, great giants of American Literature came out of the Golden Age of Publishing: Scribner's and Knopf and Maxwell Perkins editing Hemingway, Fitzgerald and Wolfe. There were interesting things going on in the contemporary narrative world populated by Barthelme, Coover, Pynchon, Hawkes and DeLillo, but if such writers challenged narrative norms they certainly demonstrated no taste for rebellion against the world of corporate publishing. Why would they? It didn't seem so corporate, for starters. In the 60s and early 70s we were hopeful about many things.

Lawrence Ferlinghetti was doing fascinating things with his Beat colleagues in San Francisco, but who knew what to make of that? One man as poet, publisher, and bookseller? Was that even legal?

As an undergraduate on scholarship I stood at the shelves of Hillel Stavis' all-night bookstore in Harvard Square at 3 a.m. and read every page of every Pocket Poets edition I could get my hands on: Patchen, Corso, Rexroth, the holy man Ginsberg, and Ferlinghetti himself. But fair Harvard did its level best to persuade me that they were outliers.

I was fiction editor of the college literary magazine my junior year. I remember an *Advocate* staff meeting one evening that Spring when I boldly, and I'm sure pretentiously, opined that we had become a tad stodgy (a tad? Hah!) and proposed we should devote an entire issue to "experimental writing."

"How will we know it's experimental?" asked a young poet named Peggy.

For all its logic, the question seemed so obtuse that I stood there unable to answer. All I could think of, somehow, was Bunsen burners.

My colleagues and classmates from the *Advocate*, from my poetry writing class with Robert Lowell and my "craft of fiction" classes with Monroe Engel and Kurt Vonnegut went on, usually with stunning turnaround times after leaving campus, to publish books by the fistful with major American publishers. I went off to organize poor people in the South, mumbling something along the way about needing to live my life before I would have anything to write about. Organizing was a good thing, but by the time a national network of citizen groups honored me as its "organizer of the year" when I was in my early 30s, most of my college writing classmates were on their third books. With the quiet regret of someone who has been entirely responsible for a colossal miscalculation, I concluded that my time as a writer had come and gone.

Almost 20 years later, I was running the day-to-day operations of Inc. magazine's ancillary books-video-software publishing division when a serious life crisis gave me the time to return to writing and the need to begin deriving income from it for the first time since I'd worked my way through college as a stringer with the Boston Globe. Call me arrogant, but after surveying the lay of the land in publishing, I decided I didn't care to subject my work to the literary judgment of the 23-year-old interns to whom usually fell the job of disposing of agents' and editors' slush piles.

Gradually I began to realize how much I knew about publishing, and to figure out how to turn my knowledge into my own practical publishing success. I published a book of short fiction in 2000 only to have it gather dust by the caseload in my basement. Every self-publishing author ought to be allowed one costly ego-driven mistake. Mine cost me about $2,000, but within a year I had formed my own publishing company. With the help of a great guy named Tom Campbell at King Printing in Lowell, Massachusetts, I went to school on the intricacies of short-run publishing and I brought out my first nonfiction book, which quickly turned a short-term profit of over $10,000 for less than a month's work. In 2002 I followed with two books about the bookselling business; together they have gone through six printings and continue to provide a steady income.

All well and good, but somewhere along the way something clicked for me, as it has for many other writers. Confronted with the occasional stigma around self-publishing – never more grating than when it came from self-styled "indie" booksellers – I will admit to becoming a tad defiant at times. But there was also something very positive and liberating about going the independent route, something that I share with many other independent authors and, I hope, with you. Once I realized that I could take creative and commercial control of my own work, it was like flipping a switch to unleash my own creative energies. The success or failure of a book would depend on things I could control, or at least influence strongly:

· the quality of my work;

· the polishing of the final package, from cover design to title to production quality to editorial and promotional copy;

· the suitability of my book to the reading interests of some significant group, or "niche," of book buyers;

· my ability to locate that niche and find specific and appropriate ways to connect with its "members" to make them aware of my book; and

· my "best practices" attention, either directly or by delegating responsibility, to all of the associated business elements of running a small but successful publishing company, including fulfillment, customer service, accounting, etc.

My company, Harvard Perspectives Press (named after the Harvard House of Pizza and the Harvard Wine Company, two favorite institutions from my undergraduate days), is tiny, but significant to me. We have successfully published six books over the past decade. This is the seventh. Until now, each has required a substantial commitment of up-front capital. Not huge, but enough so that you check the bank balance before writing the check. Because of my past experience in the book trade, as publisher, bookseller, author, reviewer, and marketing guy, I have succeeded where many others have failed, or at least fell short of their expectations.

Return to Table of Contents

PART TWO:

CREATING
YOUR OWN SUCCESS STORY
WITH NEW TECHNOLOGIES

Chapter II.1

The Ideal Process and the Ideal Platform

If you want to write a book, you can write a book.

You knew that.

If you want to publish a book, you can publish a book.

And chances are good, if you approach every step in the process with a passionate commitment to quality, that you can publish in a way that is rewarding to you in all the important ways: creatively, financially, professionally, and in the development of a lasting and meaningful relationship with your audience, your readers.

Perhaps you didn't know that. After all, it goes against centuries of conventional wisdom that has groomed writers to submit to the hierarchies and processes of the traditional publishing industry, and to place their fates in the hands of its gatekeepers and tastemakers.

What would you design, if we were starting out today with a clean slate, as an ideal publishing platform for you as an individual author?

The questions that I have sought to answer for my own purposes, in considering whether I should commit myself and my work to one of several independent publishing processes, are probably similar to those that "the talent" in each of these fields would ask:

· would my work get fair consideration, and be judged on its merits?

·   Can independent publishing give me as good a chance at getting my work in front of my intended or natural audience as I will have if I follow the traditional publishing route and start submitting it to agents and editors?

·   Can I earn enough money with this approach to (a) break even on any production and marketing costs; (b) compensate me for the creative time I have spent on the project; (c) allow me, for instance, to pay for child care and/or quit or ratchet down my day job so I can work more regularly at my writing in the future; and/or (d) provide, for myself and perhaps for my loved ones, a higher, more secure standard of living in the future?

·   Will the determining factors for my potential success as an independently published author be more logical, understandable, and actionable for me than they would be if I follow the traditional route? (The answer to this question will clearly be different for different writers, whether one is Paris Hilton or Dave Eggers or anyone else, in part because each of us brings different strengths and weaknesses to the process and in part because each of us must consider the activities that may be necessary for commercial success in the context of how we contemplate the activities that are otherwise important in our lives, such as, possibly, continued writing).

·   Will I be able to shape and to live with the mix of positive and negative experiences to which the independent route may expose me, as opposed to those that I would find on a more traditional path, with respect to notoriety and stigma, my stature with an relationships with audience and colleagues, my access to any platforms that might help to extend the reach of my writing or expression in the future, and my ability to continue working and thinking originally and creatively?

If you anticipate that you are about to be discovered, that your work will soon be snapped up and published after an agent's auction with a six-figure contract and more for the film rights, and that you will then continue to proceed inexorably along the path to riches, indie publishing may not be for you.

There may be levels of grandeur at which indie publishing cannot compete.

But if your purchase on these questions is more modest, and you are willing to work hard and intelligently at all the steps involved, and even to help to build an indie movement in which you would seek to thrive, the independent approach may be a great and important fit for you, one which will involve only moderate risks while it provides you with a real chance to make a viable career of writing.

A real chance -- and this is the headline -- for your own talent and hard work and good judgment as a writer, augmented by a pragmatic willingness to promote your work, to determine how well you succeed.

That's really all any of us have a right to hope for, but it is far more than most of us can reasonably expect from the traditional publishing industry as it has lately been configured.

Changes in technology during the past decade have effected a partial transformation in the book publishing industry. With the emergence of digital short-run book publishing, it is now possible for individuals to bring out their own books for less than $5,000 in production costs. Large numbers of writers have embraced this process: there are now about 300,000 new titles published each year.

Although most of these new titles never make it onto the shelves of physical bookstores, marketplace changes have provided authors and independent publishers with other important selling venues. Most importantly, Amazon itself has opened the doors for authors and publishers to place their work on its virtual shelves and use the powerful marketing infrastructures of online bookselling and online search to connect with readers. Going an enormous step further, Amazon has established, with the Kindle and CreateSpace, high-functioning platforms that allow authors to circumvent most publisher functions entirely and to connect their work with readers at little or no expense.

The problem, of course, is that most of this content, whether in the form of books, e-books, or articles in digital form, seldom finds readers. The vast majority of the newly published titles sell fewer than 100 copies.

The result is that tens of thousands of writers are throwing away their time and their work is going unread. It may be harsh to say "throwing away." After all, financial return on investment should never be the only or even the primary reason for publishing a book. But nearly any good reason for publishing a book should be built upon the hope and expectation that people will read the book. Even if the primary motivation is the well-deserved pride that an author feels at completing a manuscript and then being able to hold it in hand in book form, that pride is likely to attenuate rather quickly if one fails to experience the satisfaction of connecting with audience or the economic support the comes with one's work finding buyers.

In suggesting that there is another route, and furthermore that this other, independent, nontraditional route is the better way for the majority of writers (as well as being far better in the long run for readers), I do not mean to make a cheap, off-hand assertion. Independent publishing is not for hacks. It is not a get-rich-quick scheme for overzealous entrepreneurs and narcissists. It is a delicate process that requires, to repeat my earlier phrase, one to "approach every step in the process with a passionate commitment to quality." Throughout the process one must be able to maintain an almost Zen-like balance between one's creative sensibility and the nuts and bolts of marketing strategy and tactics and basic business practices, between the stars in the heavens and the cracks in the sidewalks.

Whatever value this book may have as a guide, it is just as importantly an attempt to provide a real-world context for independent publishing early in the 21st Century, to state the terms of its importance for writers and readers, and to help all of us who are passionate about indie publishing – and about the continued development of an independent literature – to frame our approach to it at least for the short term. Ideally it will provide this framework, and perhaps even a bridge of faith, for those who may at first see indie publishing as, in one way or another, a threat to what they currently do, or to the positions that they currently hold, in the book trade.

In that process, naturally, I should have a couple of things to say about the "how-to" dos and don'ts of independent publishing. And I do.

So let's talk about what you will need to succeed.

First, and most important, you need a very, very good manuscript. It must be wonderful, or very useful, or full of surprises or laughter or sadness or wisdom or information, or all of the above. It must be very well written, well edited, well organized, and well polished. This is the creative process.

Second, you need to have a very clear idea of who will read the book, why they will read it, why they will want to comment about it passionately and positively to their colleagues and friends, and how – exactly, practically how – you will contact them or otherwise get their attention in significant numbers with a persuasive message to set this essentially viral process inexorably in motion. This is the promotional part of the marketing process.

Third, until very recently you would have needed to arrange as economically, efficiently and quickly as possible for the production and warehousing of thousands of copies of your book in an attractive, professional, credible, high-impact package that will mesh seamlessly with and be integral to the promotional process. This was product design, development, and production, but its terms have changed radically to allow you two important alternatives to bulk production: wireless or other transmission of electronic "copies" of your book, and rapid "just-in-time" print-on-demand production synchronized with distribution channels that provide seamless linkage with effective marketing tools.

Fourth, you need to link these "production" and "warehousing" functions to an efficient, high-quality, prompt, and economical system for order and payment processing, fulfillment and customer service, wholesaler and retailer placement and co-marketing, return management, accounts receivable and collections, and inventory and production planning. This is the distribution portion of marketing. And again, Amazon's new platforms now make these steps seamless and automated.

These are the basic elements of the independent publishing process. Mediocrity, sloppiness, or weakness in any of these key areas will be enough to doom your overall efforts to failure.

It may not be easy for "the writer in you" to see herself focusing on production details, or ISBN registration, or the organization of your warehousing, fulfillment and distribution channels. Sure, James Joyce may have self-published *Ulysses*, but did he have to source bar codes, price shipping labels, and manage returns? Fortunately, publishing platforms such as the Kindle and CreateSpace remove almost all of this drudgery (as well as the expense) from the process.

Once you establish your publishing plan, it behooves you to create a project flow chart defining each of the tasks and professional roles involved in bringing your publishing project to fruition and then maintaining it successfully as a business enterprise. Whether you are one person acting solo, an entrepreneur envisioning some hiring and delegation, or a new literary collective looking to organize for your first publishing project, it is wise to take a formal approach to this planning process so that you have a clear sense of what you are getting into.

Equally important, I strongly advise against anyone planning to pursue a do-it-yourself independent publishing approach just once. As with most things that are worth doing, there is a learning curve. You will probably be able to do a much better job at managing and carrying out these key tasks the second time around, and even the third. In the process, of course, you will also be establishing not only your own reputation or brand identity but your own "database" of resources, contacts, and readers who will give you a leg up on the process after your initial efforts.

Chapter II.2

A Step-by-Step Approach to Publishing a Kindle Edition of Your Book or Document

After a decade of interesting but ultimately failed efforts by various electronics manufacturers to hit the sweet spot of potential for an electronic book reader, Amazon launched the Kindle reader in November 2007. Although the Kindle quickly attracted critics and naysayers who predicted failure for the device, they failed to understand how well Amazon is positioned to achieve dazzling success. Amazon's relationships with readers, early adopters, authors, and publishers provide the company with tremendous advantages over any competitor that might consider bringing an e-book reader to market, and Amazon has not squandered its opportunity. The device sold out about five hours after launch, sold over 200,000 units in its first six months (based on figures released by its Taiwan-based display-screen manufacturer), and is unlikely to look back after it reaches the one-million mark in Kindle units in circulation sometime early in 2009.

Anyone with a U.S. bank account can publish Kindle editions of books, articles or other documents for which he owns the publishing rights. You set your own price for the Kindle edition at the time of publication, and Amazon pays you 35% of the retail list price for electronic "copies" sold in each calendar month about 60 days after the close of the month. The allowable range in which you may set a Kindle edition price ranges from 99 cents up to $199.99.

However, it would be shortsighted to see that revenue or royalty as the main or only reason to publish a Kindle edition. Getting your work out there in Kindle form may help build readers for all your writing efforts during this time of publishing-industry transition. In time, of course, it could also lead to significant Kindle revenue.

With previously unpublished work, publishing a Kindle edition either of an entire book or an appropriate excerpt can be beneficial as a way of market-testing the project. Such a strategy can help you either to decide for or against going ahead with publishing on your own or to provide a traditional publisher with evidence that the project is advance-worthy.

Publishing a Kindle edition of your book or document is both free and relatively easy, but as with everything else you do as a writer, it is important to do things the right way from the start. Once you put your writing out there on the Web, it is likely to remain out there permanently, even if you attempt to pull it back. Even if you view a project as a test, putting out something that is shoddy, sloppy, or otherwise not up to your own standards can offend readers and do irreparable damage to your reputation as a writer.

Getting things right for the Kindle applies, of course, to the usual processes of manuscript preparation and your insistence on excellence. Equally important, however, are the initial processes of setting up your Kindle Edition in ways that will help you and Amazon to market your book or document effectively over the long haul. Items that need special care here include choosing a title and subtitle, selecting the content categories under which your title will be listed, writing a description of the title, setting a retail price and establishing the search keywords under which your title will be searchable in Amazon's Kindle inventory and, ultimately, elsewhere on the web as well.

Because these matters are so critically important to your success as a Kindle author, it is essential that you prepare off-line for the process of following the steps below. Open a word processing file (or get out a yellow legal pad, if you prefer), and go through the publishing steps to prepare the content that you will use before you post it. This content will very likely be some of the most important marketing content you ever write for your Kindle edition, so it is well worth a little extra time.

Many of these steps will correspond closely to the steps that you will take to publish content on Amazon's CreateSpace platform and other publishing platforms or to list, post, or register your titles for retail, wholesale, and cataloguing purposes, so it is essential to maintain and optimize all of the files and "copy" that you create as you complete this process, to help save steps, and time, later.

You shouldn't compose your search keyword lists on the Amazon screens any more than you should write a novel on the Amazon screens. In addition to the fact that drafting this material off-line will allow you to edit, revise and improve it, it also carries the extra benefit of allowing you to save the material in document form so that you can use it again or get it back if you somehow lose your Internet connection or your place in the process midstream. So, just to be clear, let me repeat that my suggestion is that you go through the following steps in draft form before actually entering material on Amazon's website.

1. Make a Publication Decision. Begin by deciding what you are going to publish. If you are publishing an entire book, then this is an obvious and easy decision. But don't overlook the potential for publishing articles and book excerpts as short-form documents in Kindle editions. If you are a non-fiction author or publisher, see if there are chapters that you can excerpt and price at $1.99 or so. These may not make you a lot of money, but if the content is good they may help you to connect with readers, market your books as well as other articles, and even create some advance interest in the book from which you are excerpting before it comes out. Short-form documents are ideal for Kindle, and in our ultra-searchable information society they can help you to build a platform and a higher profile in the Kindle Store and beyond. One important tip: in everything you publish as a Kindle edition, include easy-to-find links to a common website, blog, or a page where readers can find a linked bibliography of all your publications.

2. Manuscript Preparation. Prepare your manuscript in a single file document for Kindle edition publication. Your may prepare the document in any format that is supported by Amazon's Digital Text Platform, including Microsoft Word (.doc), Adobe PDF (.pdf), Plain Text (.txt), HTML (.html or .htm), Zipped HTML (.zip) or Mobi (.mobi or .prc). With simple text documents, there is no need to transfer or save the file as a PDF or HTML file, since Amazon's Digital Text Platform will take care of all the formatting and give you the opportunity to preview it before you publish your Kindle Edition.

(Please note: this "preview," strangely, is not an exact replica of how your content may appear on the Kindle. The only way to be absolutely certain that what you see is what others get is to obtain a Kindle, purchase your content, and check it out there).

With documents that include artwork or other embedded files, use a format that will fix the embedded files properly within your overall document. The ideal format for successful content conversion by Amazon's Digital Text Platform appears to occur with a Microsoft Word document that has been saved with the "Save as HTML" command, following this recommendation from Amazon: "Amazon DTP provides support for Microsoft Word .doc files. We recommend that you use 'Save As HTML' (in a filtered or simplified format, if available) [to save] your documents before uploading them. However, standard .doc files will often convert without a hitch."

3. Front Matter. Create a brief title and copyright page at the beginning of your document, if it is not already there. This page should begin with the full title and the author's full name. Below that should appear the name, city, website address and email address of the publishing company, if any, followed by two lines such as this:

First Kindle Original Edition, 2008

Finally, add the following paragraph, unless you are publishing material that you intend for the public domain:

You may wish to remove pagination from your Table of Contents and Index, since page numbers are not steadfast in Kindle documents due, among other things, to the fact that the Kindle allows a reader to change the font size in any document.

4. Hyperlinks in Your Text. If your book or document is non-fiction, consider embedding links within the document to allow Kindle readers to navigate to other websites using the wireless "Basic Web" functionality that comes with the Kindle. However, if you offer this feature, it may well be worth adding a disclaimer up front warning readers that using the links to navigate some graphic-heavy websites may result in slowing down a Kindle's operation or even freezing the device's screen (a condition that can usually be repaired by insert a tiny paper clip in the device's "reset" hole).

5. Digital Text Platform. Go to Amazon's Digital Text Platform website at http://dtp.amazon.com/mn/signin. You will see a "Welcome to Digital Text Platform - amazon.com" banner across the top of the page. On the left is a sign-in box where you can log on with your Amazon email address and password. You will also find links to "help" and "community forum" pages, which I suggest that you bookmark immediately under a "Kindle" label or folder.

6. Sign In. Sign in using your Amazon.com account, or establish a new account with a separate email address if you want to keep your Kindle edition publishing activity distinct both from your other Amazon activity and from other household members who may share your Amazon or email account. Make sure you keep track, in a secure place, of the email address and password that you establish for Amazon's Digital Text Platform. Few things are more frustrating than establishing such an account and then not being able to access it.

(Note: In future visits to your DTP account, it will usually be necessary to ensure that the computer you are using is not simultaneously signed in to another Amazon account. If it is, just sign out, then sign in to the appropriate Amazon account before you sign in to your DTP account).

7. Enter Account Information. Click on "My Account" to provide the important information that Amazon must have to pay your share of the proceeds from the sale of electronic copies of your Kindle Edition. Provide a full, official name for yourself or your company, depending on who owns the rights to the books or other documents that you will publish on Kindle. Type in a postal mailing address, select the business type from the pull-down menu, and enter the information for the bank account into which Amazon will electronically deposit your payments. You must have both the account number and the bank routing number to proceed here.

8. Add New Item. Using the navigation tabs at the top of the Digital Text Platform screen, click on "My Shelf," then "Add New Item." The first screen you will see is headed "Enter Product Details," and it is here that you enter the most important "marketing" material that will help Kindle owners and others search for and find your books and articles.

9. ISBN for Linking to Other Editions. You do not need an ISBN to publish a Kindle edition. However, if your book or article has a hard-copy version with an ISBN, you can type or paste the 10-digit version of it, with or without hyphens, in the ISBN box. This will enable Amazon to create a linked connection between the Kindle, hardcover, paperback and other versions of your document, which will help to enhance your sales and migrate the editorial, customer review, and bibliographic information between the print and the Kindle editions of your title. Keep it mind that Kindle owners are not the only people who will search for Kindle editions. Because of the high level of buzz concerning the Kindle, millions of other Amazon customers will scout for Kindle edition titles. In some cases this will lead them back to the dead-tree versions of these titles, and in other cases they will decide, on the basis of the growing Kindle selection and the lower prices for Kindle editions, that it is time to get Kindles of their own. If there is no version of your title with an ISBN, just skip the ISBN field.

10. Titles and Subtitles. Enter the full title and subtitle of your book or article in the Title field, with proper capitalization and a colon after the title, as in this example: 20 Steps to Publishing a Kindle Edition of Your Book or Document: How to Use Kindle, Amazon and the Web to Market Your Book and Connect with Readers. Yes, that's a mouthful. But that can be a good thing -- not the fact that it is a long title, but the fact that it is a logical, informative title that is dense with searchable words. Subtitles are more important than ever in publishing, because when they are optimized for web searching in general, and Amazon searching specifically, they can help take advantage of the marketing power of a website like Amazon's. Note also that, because it starts with a number, the article's title is also optimized for alphabetical listings.

11. Description. Write a professional, attractive description of your document, with copy similar to what might appear on a back cover or inside dustjacket flap. Proofread it carefully and paste it into the "Description" field. Don't exaggerate, embellish or make false claims about the document, or disappointed readers will be sure to retaliate with negative reviews. If the article is excerpted from a longer book, mention the book but make it clear that an excerpt is being offered here. Include a one-liner from a review if it would be helpful, with accurate quoting and attribution, of course. A brief biographical sketch of the author may also be appropriate. Amazon will force you to be succinct, since the Description field is limited to 850 characters, or about 175 words.

12. Publisher, Language and Pub Date. Enter the name of the document's publisher in the "Publisher" field. This may be either an individual or a publishing company. However, if you are approaching this question for the first time, give it some thought. If you are publishing content that requires or deserves some gravitas, calling your publishing company "Jack's Publishing" may not help. You may also want to consider using your publishing company's URL in this field, as an easy way to lure prospective readers to a website or blog where you can list other titles and provide more information.

Enter the language in which your content appears under "Language" and the publication date under "Pub Date." If your content has been published elsewhere previously, enter the original publication date. With nonfiction this is a matter, among other things, of truth in advertising, because some non-fiction work can obviously become outdated over time. If your work is appearing for the first time, the Kindle Store will automatically enter the date the item is being published once everything has been processed.

13. Content Categories. Carefully select the Kindle content categories that Amazon will use to help readers find your content. Category headings such as these are different from keywords that you invent for your title. You are only allowed 5 categories, and they must all come from Amazon's tree structure of category and subcategory headings. When you see a plus sign next to a category, you can click on it to find subcategories. Study the choices and try to imagine the categories that your readers would be most likely to use if they were hunting for a book or article like yours. Don't try to trick the system, but do be open to spreading the field a bit by thinking about different types of appeal that your article might have. For instance, the keywords for this chapter, if it were a stand-alone article, might include "Writing" as well as "Marketing," two categories that appear in different areas of the category tree structure.

The value of well-chosen categories will become especially evident later when a few sales of your Kindle edition can help to send it on a rapid ascent up the category-specific Amazon Sales Ranking ladders, thus giving you access to valuable real estate in Amazon's online store for readers who are searching your specific categories.

14. Contributors. Under "Authors," enter the names of the people who contributed to your content, including authors, editors, illustrators, translators, and individuals who wrote an introduction or preface. Although this may seem straightforward, one thing that is often overlooked is the importance of entering an author's name exactly as it may appear elsewhere in Amazon's catalogue. Since Amazon automatically hyperlinks author names, this consistency is essential if you want to make it easy for readers to find multiple works by the same author.

15. Search Keywords. The importance of what you enter in the field called "Search Keywords" cannot be overstated, so take the time to prepare well and get the most out of this. As you are certainly aware, Amazon's success as an online bookseller owes much to its success in making it easy for customers to search for the content they want, and to view Amazon's suggestions for items they may want based on past purchases, on the Amazon website. There are thousands of web marketing experts whose primary activity is to optimize web pages for search engines from Amazon's to Google's to many others so that web browsers, surfers and seekers will be able to find specific clients' products, content and activities on the web. Amazon's ability to generate sales for the content you post for Kindle depends mightily on your success at entering the most suitable keywords in the "Search Keywords" field.

The key to successful search keyword selection lies in your ability to zero in on the overlapping "sweet spot" at the intersection of two imaginary circles. In one circle, imagine words and very short phrases that would be likely choices to direct searchers to your book, article or other content. In a second circle, imagine the most popular and effective search keywords that people enter to find content on the Amazon website. Where the two circles overlap, you have search words that stand a reasonable chance of actually bringing significant traffic to your content. And unlike Google Adwords, Amazon won't charge you an advertising premium for hitting the sweet spot.

As you have probably already guessed, there are entire books on this process. Amazon's recommendation is that you select 5 to 7 individual words or very short phrases to populate the "Search Keywords" field. To help develop your understanding of how the process works, try experimenting with the free Google Adwords Keyword Tool online at https://adwords.google.com/select/KeywordToolExternal. Additionally, check for new resources and services at the indieKindle website at http://indiekindle.blogspot.com/.

16. Other Bibliographic Information. Populate the fields for "Edition Number," "Series Title," and "Volume Number." Amazon's instructions for edition number are to enter a simple number, e.g., "1," to denote whether this is the first published version of your content or a revised version. A series title might refer either to the serial name, such as "A Series of Unfortunate Events," or to an imprint title denoting a specific thematic preoccupation, such as "Harvard Perspectives in Entrepreneurship." Volume numbers are intended for magazines, journals or full-length works in a series.

17. Product Image. Upload an appropriate cover image in the "Product Image" field. A cover image of a hard-copy edition of your work is suitable here, and can help generate interest in your content just as covers attract browsers in bookstores. Your product image must be in TIFF (.tif/.tiff) or JPEG (.jpeg/.jpg) format, and must be at least 500 pixels on the longest side. If you do not have a hard-copy edition of your book, it may be worthwhile to design and digitize a product image so that you can upload it here to enhance the browsing experience. It is not strictly necessary, however, and you may also add an image at any time after you have published your content as a Kindle edition.

18. Save or Change Product Details. As you are following each of the above steps it is helpful to click on the "Save Entries" button after each step. This will help to ensure that you do not lose material. It is also worth noting that the Amazon Digital Text Platform can respond in a confusing fashion if you exceed the maximum number of allowable characters in the "Description" field. The Platform may simply fail to accept your content, or alternately may truncate the content at about 850 characters. Make sure that you draft and save your Description content off-line so that it will be easy for you to edit and pare down the content if you run a little long. Once you have saved all of your entries on the Product Details screen you can proceed to the other two primary sections of the Digital Text Platform, where you will upload and preview your book or document, set its price, and publish it. You can change your product details any time by returning to the My Shelf tab on the Digital Text Platform "Dashboard". In order to change your product details later, just click the plus [+] sign next to "Enter Product Details" for a title, change your entries or add new information, and click "Save entries". If your item has already been published, click "Publish again" to update the details in the publication.

19. *Upload and Preview Your Content*. Once your manuscript is has been subjected to careful proofreading, editing, and formatting, it is very easy to upload it. Under "Upload and Preview Book", just click on the "Browse" button and locate the file. Take the time to make sure you have located the correct draft or version of your content, and then click on "Upload," and the process begins. Most documents require just a few moments to upload, if you have a broadband Internet connection. Once the upload is complete, the Digital Text Platform will display a message informing you that your content has been successfully uploaded and converted. Once this message is displayed, it is well worth your time and effort to complete a thorough preview to look for formatting errors or editing deficiencies. You can go back to your document on your own computer, make necessary changes, and upload it again as many times as are necessary to get your document into perfect shape.

20. *Set Your Price*. The final step before you click on the "Publish" button is to set a price for your content. Setting prices is always a complex process that must take into consideration issues such as value, competition, marketing and cost. Early indications are that Amazon is setting Kindle edition prices roughly equivalent to one-third to one-half of hardcover list princes, but this may change. Check other content prices in the

Kindle Store and set your price as you see fit, knowing that you will have no ongoing production costs for Kindle editions and that your "profit" or "author royalty" will amount to 35% of the retail list price that you set. You can always change your price later. (It is worth noting that the Kindle Store frequently applies a 20% discount to the retail list price that you set for a title. This discount does not lower the amount that you will be paid, but since it lowers the purchase price, the net effect is that the royalty that you will receive amounts to about 44% of the actual purchase price when a 20% discount is applied).

Once you have completed these 20 steps, both in preparation and "live" on Amazon's Digital Text Platform, you should be ready to publish your content successfully. All it takes now is a single click of the "Publish" button, and your content should be live in 12 to 72 hours. Be patient within this time frame, and also expect that it will probably take longer for your cover graphics, bibliographic, category, editorial, and sales ranking material to appear on the title's detail page in the Kindle Store. You should also anticipate that there will be a lag of a day or so, after your title spears on its new page before customers can purchase and download it.

Good luck!

Chapter II.3

Publishing Your Fiction on the Amazon Kindle Platform: Tips and Tactics For Helping Kindle Readers to Connect With Novels and Short Stories

As we have discussed in the previous chapter, the user-friendly search environment of the Kindle Store makes it especially well suited for topical nonfiction publishing. If you publish quality nonfiction books and articles that provide useful information for specific niche markets of readers and do a good job of optimizing your listing for search, readers will find your work.

But how about fiction? Given the untold millions who are out there working on the next Great American Novel, or working hard to be the next Richard Ford, Sue Miller, or Sherman Alexie, how can fiction writers possibly distinguish their work among the thousands of books in the Kindle Store?

Obstacles

To be honest, it isn't easy to get readers interested in new sources of fiction. We are up against several forces:

* There's a lot of mediocre fiction out there, and many readers retreat into a posture of protecting themselves by sticking with particular authors who are tried, true, or previously vetted by Oprah.

* Despite the fact that the lion's share of the aforementioned mediocre fiction is issued by the corporate mega-publishers, many readers begin with a bias against independently or self-published fiction. Instead, they assume that "if it is published by Simon & Schuster, it must be good." The corollary, of course, is that they stigmatize self-published fiction.

* It is virtually impossible to get traditional book reviewers to touch anything that isn't published in dead-tree book form by a traditional publisher. Without reviews, fiction by emerging authors is even less likely to attract readers' attention.

* The old "so many books, so little time," conundrum that afflicts most of us, along with its financial corollary.

Worst of all, writers -- most writers, but especially fiction writers and poets -- are constantly held to an impossible and counter-productive standard with respect to any efforts they might make to promote or market their work. Doctors and lawyers can advertise, pro athletes can compete against amateurs in the Olympics, blockbuster authors can benefit from their publishers' full-page ads and financially lubricated book tours, but somehow there has been little movement in the cultural prohibitions that informed Emily Dickinson's line to the general effect that "publication is not the business of poets," or emerging independent writers of any other stripe.

Key Elements to Help Build Readership for Fiction

But I have been holding my finger up in the air waiting for an indie breeze for some time now, and I believe it is beginning to rustle the leaves a bit. I also believe in the potential of the Kindle as one force among many that could help to foster an "indie movement" revolution in publishing and in the connection between authors and readers, perhaps somewhat similar to what we have seen in music and film.

So it is far from impossible to build readership for independently fiction and poetry on the Kindle. Based on what I have observed, there are several elements that can be helpful, and in some cases essential, in this process:

* First and foremost, it must be quality work. Otherwise, even a temporary bump in sales will be followed by negative or unenthusiastic customer reviews in the Kindle store and the main Amazon site, and in most cases sales will decline accordingly.

* The author (or somebody acting on the author's behalf) must be willing to do some promotion. If you believe that it is beneath you to market your work or to provide a boost to the process of generating buzz for it, that reticence will probably be reflected in your sales.

* It is extremely valuable to have a platform as an author: a pre-existing reputation or position that can help you to create public awareness for your book. Many authors are too quick to define themselves out of this category because they do not have a radio or television program, a newspaper or magazine column, or a previous bestseller. But platforms can come in many forms, and if you have a blog, a following, a position in your community, or any "base" that allows you to make easy, non-spamming contact with a significant group of potential readers, you may be surprised at how helpful it can be to your book sales.

Using Keywords with Fiction

Use keywords creatively to help readers find your fiction. When you read about keywords earlier in the previous chapter, you may have skipped over it with the thought that such a device would apply only to nonfiction. It is certainly true that the search process and keywords come into play more often with nonfiction, but you should certainly take advantage of their potential for helping readers find your fiction. Here are a few suggestions for types of keywords that could work well with fiction:

* Bibliographic: Include your title, author's name, and the Amazon categories under which you have listed your title, as well as any other Amazon categories or genre information that you were not able to find or use in the Categories field.

Amazon search categories and Amazon keywords are not an either-or proposition. Think of them as two columns on the same page that can work symbiotically to assist readers in finding your work, and don't hesitate to build in some redundancy, or even some duplicative redundancy, between the two columns.

* Make search keywords out of the names of key characters, places, topics and subject matter of your fiction. If you have written a novel about identity theft, fratricide, nanotechnology, baseball or some other topical terrain that is likely to show up in Amazon reader searches, help readers find it, even if they happened to begin their searches looking for nonfiction. One important tip based on the general principles of search engine optimization: any word or phrase that you use as a keyword should also occur elsewhere on your title's Kindle detail page, either in the title, subtitle, description or in the standard bibliographic information that you provide, so that search crawlers will not discount your keywords as an effort to trick the search engines.

* If your title's editorial description says that your book evokes the novelist Richard Ford or will make readers think of the dialogue from the film Fargo, don't be shy. Go ahead and extend the name-dropping to the keywords field.

Seeing What Works:
Examples of Independent Fiction Writers' Success

There is no single formula for achieving success in connecting good fiction with Kindle readers, but one of the most fruitful exercises for any of us to watch what others are doing and to make a note of what works. So let's take a few moments to break down some useful promotional efforts that have worked well for others on the Kindle platform. I'll start with a few experiences of my own, since they are by far the most modest in their success, and we will work toward a crescendo with the subsequent discussions of novelists Daniel Oran and April L. Hamilton.

Stephen Windwalker

As you may have noticed, I have recently been hard at work on two nonfiction books; this article is an excerpted chapter from one of them. However, as with many other authors, nonfiction is the day job that allows me to pursue my primary creative passion, writing fiction. Historically I have maintained a not very rigid line between the two activities by publishing most of my nonfiction under my pen name, Stephen Windwalker, and writing fiction under the name my parents gave me, Steve Holt.

With the Kindle platform, I quickly realized that I could earn a significant income with some future, current and past nonfiction projects, while I also could publish my fiction without having to lay out thousands of dollars to a printer or submit myself to the literary tastes of some 23-year-old intern at a traditional publishing house. The nonfiction, I knew, would sell much better unless some particular work of fiction happened to catch fire at some point. But it also made sense to me to try dropping the distinction between my given name and my pen name, so that the significantly larger numbers of readers who bought my nonfiction titles would at least have a chance to find my fiction if the spirit moved them to conduct an author search.

Long story short, this strategy has achieved mild success. Several weeks ago I listed a couple of fiction titles for Kindle readers. I published a short story for children, called "The Circle in the Forest," under the name Stephen Windwalker. At around the same time I published a novel, *Say My Name*, under my given name, Steve Holt. I haven't had any time to promote either title beyond the work that I put into the listings themselves. The story published under the Windwalker name has sold several copies a week and generally occupied a perch somewhere between 5,000 and 25,000 in the Kindle Store sales rankings. The novel has averaged a single sale per week. Although this is too small a sample to use as a basis for drawing much of a conclusion, it seems to confirm the rather obvious notion that -- where Kindle sales are concerned -- a rising tide may lift any other boats that are in your one particular harbor.

Naturally, if I want my fiction to find an active readership, I will eventually have to do more than simply affix my pen name to it. But the simple lesson here is that there is something to be said for being prolific, for publishing various kinds of work on the Kindle platform, and for making one's different titles and categories easy to connect with, and search from, one another. An equally important step that follows from this experience is to streamline one's website, blog, AmazonConnect author profile/blog/bibliography, or other informational hubs so that readers or browsers of *one* of your titles are seamlessly provided with the opportunity to browse, to read, or to buy your other titles in any categories where have you produced published work.

Daniel Oran and *Believe*

When Jeff Bezos appeared on the Charlie Rose program on the day of the Kindle's launch, he had some interesting things to say about new and old approaches to publishing with the Kindle, from serialization of novels to publishing books for subscribers:

"Why wouldn't that happen? We've always seen that when you have a new technology or new medium, it can create a new art form or sometimes re-enliven old ones as in the case of the Charles Dickens serialization. But when you have a wireless device like this, you know, we're not doing this today, but why couldn't an author decide, 'Look, I'll sell a subscription to the book, instead of selling the book. You can download it as I write. It'll automatically be delivered to your Kindle....' These are the kinds of things that are possible.

"I personally believe that there will be many, many experiments done over time. I think most of those experiments will fail. I mean, they won't be that interesting. But the great thing is that a high level of experimentation will lead to a few winners.... We may get a return to the Dickens serialization, or something else that's not even been thought of yet."

It was very much in the spirit of Bezos' remarks, about five weeks later, that Daniel Oran posted the following on his AmazonConnect blog for the Kindle edition of his new novel *Believe*:

Beta testing a novel

12:48 PM PST, December 27, 2007, updated at 9:30 PM PST, January 14, 2008

This is a publishing experiment, made possible by the new Amazon Kindle.

In the old days, BK (before Kindle), it was hard for a writer to collect much feedback on a novel in progress. Even the most forbearing friends and family eventually tire of reading yet another draft of the same story.

With Kindle, though, the audience of potential helpers is enormous. Just the way that Google (or Amazon) can invite the public to preview an early, "beta" version of a new service, a writer can now offer the draft of a novel to curious readers.

Of course, since the mid-nineties, the Web itself has made possible that kind of mass distribution and interaction. What's different about Kindle?

For most people, reading a few hundred pages on a computer screen is uncomfortable. And printing a few hundred pages for later reading is a chore.

So Kindle -- with its complete solution of wireless distribution, easy on-screen reading, and painless payment -- is a quantum leap over merely posting a file on a Web server and hoping for the best.

This draft of the novel is what the software industry might call a "late beta" -- version 0.9, at an affordable price of $0.99 -- just about ready for the bookstore.

I hope you'll give it a try, then share your feedback in an Amazon review.

During this beta test, I'm donating all of the proceeds to the Neediest Cases Fund, which helps deserving individuals and families in New York City. (You can learn more at nycharities.org/neediest.)

Thank you very much.

Daniel Oran

believebeta @ yahoo.com

Did it work? Oh my, did it work. Kindle owners began buzzing about the book in the forums and on Kindle blogs, and within a day or two the book jumped up to #7 on the Kindle Store's bestseller list! Along the way, it didn't hurt to get free publicity like these two posts on the Amazon Kindle blog that counts thousands of Kindle owners among its regular readers:

Read the Book Before the Publishers

9:27 AM PST, January 10, 2008, updated at 12:04 PM PST, January 12, 2008

*We recently came across something we think is really cool and fun. Author Daniel Oran is using Kindle to let early readers help him refine a draft of his latest book, **Believe**. Oran, a former Microsoft employee whose name still exists on the Windows 95 "Start menu" patent, is now a full-time writer. Bypassing the traditional route of garnering early feedback from agents and editors, Oran will benefit from helpful comments from the people who really count for commercial fiction -- fiction readers. For 99 cents, you can download and read the beta version of Oran's manuscript on your Kindle and offer feedback on the book's physical page. Tell him what you liked, what you think could be improved, or simply give it a "thumb's up." All proceeds go to charity.*

Via email, Oran responded to our questions on his beta test: "I published my first novel the old-fashioned way: agent, publisher, bookstores, etc. And I was struck by how one-sided the process was: the primary feedback from readers came in the form of sales figures. This time, I wanted a more interactive process -- with feedback from readers before the final version was shipped to bookstores. Fortuitously, Kindle appeared just as I was finishing up my second novel. It provided exactly what I was looking for. I still plan to go the traditional route eventually, with a regular paper version of my novel. But, with Kindle, I think there's a new first step available, involving the writer and the reader in a conversation that couldn't have taken place in quite this way even a few months ago. And I suspect that it's just the beginning of a real revolution in the relationship between writers and readers. I want this novel to be as engaging and entertaining as I can possibly make it, so this kind of mass pre-publication feedback will be really valuable."

And, a few weeks later:

Kindle-izing It

12:36 PM PST, February 7, 2008, updated at 1:13 PM PST, February 7, 2008

*One of my favorite Kindle features is getting some recognition. After spending years in publishing and seeing some of the most promising manuscripts wilt in slush piles under an editor's desk, I've become a strong proponent of digital publishing. Last month, we posted on Daniel Oran's beta test--Oran posted his work-in-progress **Believe** (only one more day to download this title for 99 cents, all of which goes to charity) to the Digital Text Platform and asked readers for feedback. The book made it to number 7 in the Kindle bestseller rankings and Oran said he received "some great feedback on the novel during the beta test -- in reviews, blog comments, and email -- so now it's time to work on a revised draft."*

To our absolute delight, Oran reported that he was contacted just this morning by a publisher in New York showing interest in publishing a paper version of Believe. Oran said of his experience: "It's a testament to the amazingly cool platform that Amazon has created!" Good luck, Danny, we're rooting for you.

And our favorite quote from a blogger at [TheBookseller.com]: "No one has noticed yet one of the biggest features: they have set up DTP Amazon that allows anyone to publish their work for the Kindle. This is a leap on from Lulu.com because there is no printing or delivery costs and transfer is trouble-free and almost instant. The DTP aspect will be a massive self-supporting market in itself as people self-publish and then make their friends buy a copy. It could also transform publishing, as authors cut out all the middlemen except for advertising agencies. Even if this method of publication only works for the obscure unpublished author, that will be great. We think of self-publishers as naive/vain hobbyists, but the long tail contains a lot of great content that just doesn't fit inside the financial model of the current industry. Plenty of great poets only exist for us thanks to self-publishing. I think the kindle could allow us to access more talent previously hidden by economic realities."

Maybe you're the next Melville or Morrison. Visit the Digital Text Platform at http://dtp.amazon.com/mn/signin and show the world what ya got. --Molly

Well, what can I add to this? It's probably worth breaking things down a bit, with the following observations:

* Pricing **Believe** at just 99 cents definitely had a salutary affect on sales of the title. And of course, once Oran decided to donate all the proceeds to charity, it didn't have any negative effect on his revenues that his share of the sales was only 35 cents per unit. (I hope this doesn't seem snarky; I'm just trying to point out that a lot more people are likely to take a chance on an unknown quantity if the price is under a buck, compared with $10.)

* Once the title cracked the top 10 and got the free publicity quoted above, it was flying above the radar so that it was highly noticeable for Kindle readers. The top 10 titles are always in view on the main page of the Kindle store. Whenever a customer buys a Kindle title on his computer, the "Thank You" screen that appears next shows a list of the top 5 titles in the Kindle store alongside another list of titles purchased by customers who had purchased whatever title the customer just

bought. And the #1 top seller in the Kindle Store is always highlighted, all by itself, on the main "Shop in Kindle Store" screen right on the Kindle device, which is obviously the very definition of prime real estate, and it is free – all you have to do is get there. Success breeds success.

Even if you are planning to charge $5 to $10 eventually, starting out with a price of 99 cents can provide a helpful assist as you try to climb the sales ranking ladder toward the exclusive real estate in the top 10. If Oran gets a book contract out of the experience, it is bound to compensate for whatever he lost in a few weeks of Kindle royalties.

* It's unclear, of course, whether Oran really hoped for a lot of feedback and "workshopping" help with his novel. In the first two months of the experiment he sold well over a thousand copies, and he got feedback in the "reviews" from fewer than two dozen. Of course, he may have received a lot of helpful emails. Whether he did or not, the nice tone of his blog entry and its request for feedback is bound to have helped create a receptive atmosphere.

Obviously, there is no single cookbook for this kind of imaginative approach to connecting your fiction with readers via the Kindle or other platforms. If I were to suggest a single specific stratagem here I would run the risk of destroying it through over-use. But Oran's experience says a lot about the potential that the Kindle has for helping entrepreneurial fiction writers to find an audience and even, in some cases, to make a living pursuing their passion.

April L. Hamilton and *Snow Ball*

Then there's the last of my three examples, April L. Hamilton. On February 20, while procrastinating a bit about getting this chapter done, I came across a post on the Amazon Kindle forum that caught my attention immediately because its title sounded like it could easily be a chapter title from this book:

Can Kindle Revolutionize the Publishing Industry?

Initial post: Feb 20, 2008 11:20 AM PST

April L. Hamilton says:

Now that the industry is dominated by vertically-integrated publishing megaconglomerates who are only interested in books that can turn reliable, impressive profits, there's no place for the book equivalent of an indie film or indie band. Self-pub books are stigmatized and also totally shut out of the national brick and mortar bookstore distribution networks, but with ebooks authors can bypass publishers and distributors entirely to get their work directly to the reader.

The Kindle provides a unique window of opportunity in this area which has never existed before: authors can release a new book in Kindle format only, then leverage Kindle edition sales and reviews to release and promote a Print-On-Demand, paper version of the same book in the 'regular' Amazon bookstore (where its pre-existing Amazon sales figures and reviews will carry over to ALL other editions of the book). If it works, the result will be a direct author-to-reader supply and demand chain that renders the publishing house completely optional...an indie book movement.

*I'm having some success in this with my Kindle-edition novel **Snow Ball**, which has sold 29 copies and garnered 2 4-star reviews in its first week on sale (having a link to a free excerpt in the book's description seems to be a huge factor in my sales so far), but I'm having trouble finding more ways to promote it or raise its profile since there seems to be no `Booklist' or `Publishers Weekly' targeted specifically to the Kindle (yet).*

I'm trying to get high-profile Kindle owners and Kindle bloggers to review it in the meantime, but does anyone here know of any Kindle-specific, ebook-, self-pub or POD book review publications or websites?

I was game. 29 copies may not sound like much, but there are plenty of emerging novelists who would love to have such a start. I downloaded the two-chapter "free excerpt," sent it wirelessly to my Kindle, and read it. I liked it. I bought the Kindle edition of April's book for $3.99, began reading it, and gave it a favorable review. On the Kindle Discussion Forum's "What Are You Reading?" thread, I posted the following:

Windwalker Books says:

*I've just finished Sue Miller's **The Senator's Wife**, which was a terrific read, with her usual generosity toward her scarred, flawed characters and a deftly handled twist at the end.*

*I've begun reading April L. Hamilton's **Snow Ball**, an indie novel by a writer who has a great ear for dialogue -- reminds me a little bit of the film **Fargo** in the early going! -- and 3 chapters in I am very pleased with my choice. Few things make me happier than "discovering" fresh talent!*

Next up is a draft novel for which I am serving as editor. My client sent it to me as a Word document and I sent it on to my Kindle email address so that I can read it and annotate it anywhere.

I will admit that the very first thing I "read" on my Kindle was one of my own titles, but only to make sure that the interactive links were working in the Table of Contents!

Oran's **Believe** has continued to maintain strong sales and good placement in the Kindle store, whereas Hamilton's two novels have drifted gradually downward after an initial splash. The steps that all of us take to build community between authors and readers on the Kindle platform and elsewhere will pay us all back over the long haul. About a month ago I spent an entire breakfast meeting kicking around ideas with my friend Paul for a Kindle "literary magazine," of sorts. Ideally it would include plenty of reviews, some excerpts, the occasional big name alongside emerging authors, and a few pages of tips, hacks and hints appealing to all Kindle owners. Maybe it could even feature an occasional writing contest.

Who will do it? Maybe Paul and I, although it's not so clear when the work would get done. Maybe the librarian named "Jan" who has started a nice blog called The Kindle Reader. Maybe some other combination of talented, entrepreneurial go-getters.

But it should be done. And it should be just one among many steps to help make the Kindle platform work for readers and writers alike.

Whether you see the Kindle publishing opportunity as a chance to connect your work directly with readers, as a way to market-test a book project by publishing an excerpt to test response, or as a creative way to build the kind of numbers that might persuade a conventional publisher to give you a book contract, it is time for you to get started.

As a fiction writer trying to ply your trade while coping with all the competing claims of daily life in the 21st century, you probably don't have the time to be the one who starts the first Kindle literary magazine or other new, new thing. That's okay. Others will come along to do that work. But it behooves you to be the ones who watches for and engages with developments that could be helpful to you in spreading your wings and ascending into the radar zone.

10 More Tips for Promoting Your Kindle Fiction

Just in case you need another little push to get started, here are a few additional suggestions:

1. Review other authors' Kindle fiction, and sign your review with a tastefully done "signature" that references your role as author of "[title of your book]" without spamming. (While it is important that you have read any book that you review, it is not necessary to have read the Kindle edition or even to own a Kindle).

2. Send free copies of your fiction to active fiction reviewers in the Kindle store and on the main Amazon site. This may take a little sleuth work, but it could be easier than you think. Start by going to Amazon's own list of Top Reviewers. Browse through this list and you'll find that you can click on the name of each reviewer to navigate to that individual's reviews. Once you arrive there, look in the upper left corner of the page to see if there is a link to the reviewer's profile. In many cases,

you will find an email address (often doubling as the reviewer's "nickname") to which you may wish to consider sending your review copy.

3. Include "Review Copy of New Kindle Edition Fiction" or words to that effect in the subject line of your friendly, professional "cover" email along with the digital copy of your fiction. You can't send a free Kindle copy, but you can send the same file that you used to upload your title to the Kindle Digital Text Platform. Ask the reviewer if she would consider reading your work and posting a review, and include the link to the detail page of your Kindle edition so she can see your descriptive editorial and bibliographic content and easily post a review there.

4. Create your own Amazon Profile on the main Amazon website. Tailor your content to present yourself as a fiction writer and include information that you are comfortable making public. Use the AmazonConnect feature to add your own Artist Blog and a bibliography of your available titles.

5. Consider asking friends and colleagues to mention your book or story on the Kindle Customer Discussion forum. There is a fine line between spam and recommendations, and you should never make such a post yourself. If a friend, acquaintance or reader likes your work and wants to mention it favorably, there are usually current forum threads with titles such as "What are you reading now?" and "Have you published a book for the Kindle?"

6. Even better, those who admire your writing should be encouraged to write a positive review on the title's detail page in the Kindle store. They may post reviews in the Kindle store whether they have read the work in Kindle, paper or other form. The only requirement is that a reviewer must have an Amazon account under which she must previously have made at least one Amazon purchase.

7. Consider a gimmick such as a serialization or subscription offer in the Kindle platform only if your content is fully ready for publication. If you get come down with a bad case of the flu or, perish the thought, writer's block, you'll only

make your readers angry at you if you can't deliver on your deadlines. If you do experiment with serialization, the way to do it is to re-post your content with each new chapter added each week (or whatever other period), so that readers only have to pay once. The descriptive and bibliographic material must clearly state the nature of the offering and the reader's responsibility to download and refresh the content each week using the Your Media Library page in their Amazon account. You can ask readers to supply you with an email address so that you can send them a heads up each week when new content is available. Generally speaking, this kind of offer can be a tad complicated and should only be tried if you have a bit of a following to begin with and really, really know what you are doing.

8. Spend a week planning and polishing the marketing campaign for your fiction title before you post the title in the Kindle Store, so that you can hit the ground running with a fully activated arsenal of tools from the very beginning. One of the truths of selling anything anywhere on the Amazon website is that sales breed more sales because they move you up the ladder that determines how often Amazon customers see your title. Consequently, just about anything you do to market your book will have greater impact if your book is in the top 5,000 titles, and even greater if it is in the top 500.

9. While it is true that you should hit the ground running, it is equally true that you should take the long view and commit yourself to, at least, a three-year plan for marketing your book. Many eventual bestsellers take off because of word of mouth that occurs gradually as they find readers, and there have been some great fiction success stories that didn't gather real momentum until a title had been available for over a year.

10. Part of the fun and the challenge of successful publishing on the Kindle platform, for many fiction writers, is that they get to, and have to, wear all the hats involved in publishing their work. Accept your role as the primary PR flack for your book and take the job seriously. Commit some time to doing all the little things like writing a professional book proposal, an enticing description (that would double as back

cover copy on a paper version of your book), your bio and a good press release ahead of time so that you can make use of them when you begin promoting your book. These exercises, in addition to being useful marketing tools, will also help you to envision and connect with the market of readers that you seek.

Chapter II.4

Publishing Periodicals For the Amazon Kindle: What Would Poor Richard Do?

If Ben Franklin were preparing, today, to publish the first issue of *Poor Richard's Almanack*, where would he bring it? He would face the same basic equation that we all face as publishers of magazines or books: the balance between the high costs of printing, warehousing and distribution vs. the desire for wider circulation and more readers.

No doubt young Ben would understand the importance of attracting as many edgy early-adopter eyeballs as he could to take note of his wise and witty zine. So it's a no-brainer: Ben would look into the possibility of publishing his journal on Amazon's Digital Text Platform (DTP) for the Kindle e-book reader. Sure, sales might get off to a slow start on this new platform, but each month the population of Kindle owners is bound to grow. Not to mention the fact that these Kindle owners have proven their chops as readers by laying out $399 (or more) for an e-book reader.

Equally important, an entrepreneurial spirit like Ben would have faith that this very interesting Jeff Bezos character and his minions could come up with some fascinating ways for Kindlers to exchange buzz and communicate with each other about what they like, and what they don't like, from the vast and ever-growing digital catalog of reading matter available to them.

Of course the bottom line would be a critical deciding factor. The Kindle would take Ben far beyond just saving a little on the cost of ink and paper. Publishing on the Kindle platform is free! Ben would probably even be happy to offer the *Almanack* at a discount price to Kindle owners if it meant he could widen his circulation while lowering his overall printing costs.

A Magazine Publishing Work-Around for the Kindle

There's just one catch. In spite of the impressive Kindle launch, with colorful graphics on the Amazon website to display cover images of the magazines and newspapers that are already available for the Kindle, there is apparently a problem. There were 8 magazines available on the Kindle when the device launched on November 19, 2007, and there were still 8 magazines available more than 2 full months later. As I put the finishing touches on this edition in May 2008 the number of Kindle edition magazines is up to 15, but still, how can this be? Is it possible that Jeff and the Amazonians don't really want to provide more magazines?

Just when Ben was ready to start competing with *Time, Salon*, and the *New York Times*, Amazon slams the door in his face!

Or not.

Here's what the inventive Mr. Franklin would figure out next: front door, back door, or through the bathroom window, it doesn't matter.

Indeed, because the Kindle is such a flexible, user-friendly, protean platform for reading content of any length, creative, imaginative publishers, authors, bloggers, and zinesters are publishing their content for the Kindle with little regard for the old lines of demarcation between categories. (Don't get me wrong: it is extremely important to describe any Kindle content fully and accurately so that browsers and prospective readers can understand clearly what they are getting before they make a purchase, but that can be done perfectly well under the overall category of Kindle Books. The book catalog of the main Amazon website has been a great place to buy and sell magazines for years, and the same is true for Kindle Books listings of digitalized magazines).

Let's be clear from the start that the main process that we are describing here is a work-around process. As we noted above, Amazon currently lists a grand total of 15 magazines under its "Kindle Magazines" tab. An email address is also provided for those who wish to contact Amazon about adding their magazines to this list. If you wish to sell your magazine in the Kindle store, you should by all means try the front door first. Send an email expressing your interest to digitalpublications@amazon.com. However, since the list has remained at 15 since the Kindle was launched in November 2007, a work-around also seems in order, and I don't recommend waiting around for an answer before you proceed with the work-around approach. After all, it is possible that it may even be more beneficial to list your magazine's issues under the "Kindle Books" tab.

Why? If you list each issue under the Kindle Books tab, you can set specific searchable keywords and authors for each issue so that readers seeking out specific content that may appear only in a given month's issue will be better able to find it. You can set a price for each issue, and if you set it in the 99 cents to $2.99 range you may generate more net revenue than you would generate from Kindle magazine subscriptions. You can also make it easy for readers who buy a single issue of your periodical to "opt in" to an email notification from you whenever a new issue goes live in the Kindle store.

What do you lose by using this work-around approach to magazine publishing for the Kindle? There are two primary potential downsides that you should consider:

1. Kindle owners who only think to look for your title under the heading of "Kindle Magazines" will not find it there.

2. You will miss out on the regular Kindle wireless "push" of your content to subscribers that is a nice feature of an e-zine subscription.

Of course, there is a pretty good comeback for each of these potential problems:

1. Kindle owners will be able to search for your content or your title under the "Kindle Books" or "Kindle Store" heading, where they are much more likely to spend the vast majority of their browsing and searching time. Publishing each issue as a separate Kindle title also allows you to optimize each issue for search based on its individual content.

2. It should be easy to encourage interested readers to use links or instructions that you can embed in each issue to email you with an automatic request that you notify them whenever a future issue is available for free download. If a reasonable number of readers avail themselves of this opportunity, you could well experience greater revenue from recurring single-issue Kindle sales than you would experience from Kindle subscriptions.

Most importantly, with regard to both of these aforementioned problems, they are only problems in comparison to an unrealized hypothetical. When and if Amazon makes it possible for you to enter through the front door of the Kindle Magazine newsstand, it will be worth revisiting such issues. By then, if you follow the steps in this article, you will have built a track record that will assist you in evaluating how best to present your zine to Kindle owners. At that point, if Amazon were to allow me my druthers (and why wouldn't they?), I would probably opt to list my magazine -- or all but the current issue -- both ways.

Why Publish Your Zine for the Kindle?

More than any other form of the printed word, independent magazine publishing has begun to deliver on its potential as a rich and appealing creative environment similar to those created in the indie film and music movements. Unfortunately, indie magazines of all kinds have found it extremely challenging to deal with high production and distribution costs, the squeeze of limited periodical slots in bookstores and newsstands, and the difficulty of connecting with readership niches and individual readers. Now, if you are the publisher of a magazine, e-zine, newsletter or other periodical, a remarkable new opportunity has opened up to you with the launch of the Kindle. The potential is so great that one blogger has speculated that magazine publishing will be the "killer app" for the Kindle.

Killer app or not, the truth is that you can publish your magazine, e-zine or other journal on the Kindle's Digital Text Platform today: current issues, back issues, individual articles or any other form.

How much does it cost?

Nothing. Not a dime. Zilch. Naturally, it is also worth pointing out that there are no printing, warehousing, or distribution costs. All you need are the digital files of your content, preferably in Word or HTML or in a format that you can convert to Word or HTML.

Okay, it doesn't cost anything, but can you actually charge for your content and get paid for it?

Oh yes.

You set the price for any issue, document, article or book that you publish on the Digital Text Platform, anywhere in a range between 99 cents and $199.99. Amazon keeps 65% of the proceeds, and deposits the other 35% in your bank account via electronic funds transfer (EFT) approximately sixty (60) days following the end of the calendar month during which sales of your content occur, provided that your account has a positive balance of $10 or more.

If 65% sounds a little steep, remember that you don't have any printing, warehousing, distribution or other overhead costs for the "copies" you sell to Kindle owners. And, yes, Amazon is definitely in this business to make money.

Whether your goals are to connect your content with readers, make money, or both, you can achieve success if you follow the steps in this article to publish a quality magazine on the Amazon Kindle Digital Text Platform. The key ingredients for success are simple, even if they are not easy:

* you must publish a quality periodical, preferably with a regular, predictable schedule and interesting content that will appeal to a growing group of readers; and

* you must make optimal use of the powerful search and marketing tools that Amazon has built into the Digital Text Platform for the Kindle so that the maximum possible number of Kindle owners will notice your magazine, buy it, read it, and help you create buzz about it.

These are not requirements for using the platform; they are just requirements for success. As your zine grows and develops, so will Amazon's base of Kindle owners. If you can sell 150 "copies" of your zine (or any other title) on the Kindle platform next month, there is a good chance that the growth in the number of Kindles in circulation may predict sales of 500 copies a year from next month, and more than 1,000 two years out. The popularity of the Kindle and Amazon's powerful marketing infrastructure are bound to create an ever wider base of potential readers for your zine and any other content published on the Kindle platform.

Formatting Your Zine for the Kindle

If your magazine already exists as an e-zine, you have a leg up on the formatting process. But even if you have worked strictly with paper in the past, the process of preparing, formatting and uploading your content should be straightforward.

1. Prepare your content for publishing on the Digital Text Platform. Begin with your current issue and always make sure your current issue goes live as early as possible by publishing it as soon as your digital content is (or would be) ready for the

printer. Prepare as many back issues as you like for publication. Each issue will occupy its own rich, searchable detail page in the Kindle store. If you make effective use of search and keyword optimization to bring out the best in each back issue, your back issues will sell copies and also help drive traffic to your current issues.

2. Format each issue as a single HTML document. You may prepare the document in any format that is supported by Amazon's Digital Text Platform, including Microsoft Word (.doc), Adobe PDF (.pdf), Plain Text (.txt), HTML (.html or .htm), Zipped HTML (.zip) or Mobi (.mobi or .prc). With simple text documents, there is no need to transfer or save the file as a PDF or HTML file, since Amazon's Digital Text Platform will take care of all the formatting and give you the opportunity to preview it before you publish your Kindle Edition. With documents that include artwork or other embedded files, use a format that will fix the embedded files properly within your overall document. The ideal format for successful content conversion by Amazon's Digital Text Platform appears to occur with a Microsoft Word document that has been saved with the "Save as HTML" command, following this recommendation from Amazon: "Amazon DTP provides support for Microsoft Word .doc files. We recommend that you use 'Save As HTML' (in a filtered or simplified format, if available) [to save] your documents before uploading them. However, standard .doc files will often convert without a hitch."

3. Front Matter. Front matter can include an image of your cover, a title, masthead and copyright page, your Table of Contents and, if appropriate, a Notes on Contributors section.

On the copyright page, include the following paragraph, unless you are publishing material that you intend for the public domain:

All rights reserved. This document may not be reproduced in any form, in whole or in part (beyond that copying permitted by U.S. Copyright Law, Section 107, "fair use" in teaching or research, Section 108, certain library copying, or in published media by reviewers in limited excerpts), without written permission from the publisher.

Make sure that you, or any corporate entity under whose auspices you are uploading your content, own the rights to all the content that you are uploading. If there is any possibility that your periodical's contributors retain the rights to electronic publication of their work, you must negotiate with them and reach an agreement for permissions, compensation and any other outstanding issues before you publish their work in a Kindle version or any other electronic form. Applicable permissions should be noted on the copyright page.

If your magazine presents special formatting challenges above and beyond the scope of this article or the skills of your design people, it is a good idea to get assistance from a guy like Joshua Tallent, who has established a helpful website with Kindle formatting tips and also does some consulting for prospective Kindle publishers and authors.

Making the Most of Hyperlinks
In a Kindle Edition of Your Magazine

You can make the Kindle edition of your magazine much more user-friendly by building hyperlinks into your Table of Contents. The good news is that it is very easy to add such links (or any other links) to your text. It may take you an extra 20 minutes or so when you are formatting your text for publication on Kindle's Digital Text Platform, a little longer if you have yet to create a Table of Contents. You don't need a lick of HTML knowledge to do it, because the commands for adding these links is built into Microsoft Word:

1. Create a Table of Contents for your document if you haven't done so already. The Table of Contents (and other front matter) can be part of the main document, located as it would be in a paper edition. Note: If you want to use a smidgen of HTML here, you have the option of using simple HTML attribute anchor tags to set the start of your magazine's Table of Contents

-- A NAME="TOC"/ -- and the starting "reading location" -- A NAME="start"/.

2. Make sure that each title or article listing in your Table of Contents corresponds to a "heading" in the document, formatted and set off with an extra line of spacing to help Microsoft Word recognize it as a heading.

3. For each title in your Table of Contents, capture the title text (in the Table of Contents) with your mouse, right-click on the captured title text, and choose "Hyperlink" in the little dialogue box that appears on your screen.

4. Choose "Place in this document" from the four options on the left of the "Insert Hyperlink" dialogue box that appears on your screen, and select "Headings" from the choices provided.

5. When you click on "Headings," Microsoft Word will show you a list of the headings that appear in your magazine. Click on the heading that matches the Table of Contents text that you have captured, and Word automatically creates the link.

Test your links before you upload your magazine. An alternative approach to creating hyperlinks that allows greater fine-tuning and usually takes a little longer is available using the "Bookmarks" feature in the "Insert" pull-down menu in Microsoft Word. This feature is also appropriate for hyperlinking an index.

You will probably want to remove pagination from your Table of Contents and Index, since page numbers are not steadfast in Kindle documents due, among other things, to the fact that the Kindle allows a reader to change the font size in any document.

Another handy feature to include at the end of each article is a "Back to Top" or "Back to Table of Contents" link. Just use your mouse to capture a phrase such as Back to Top, right click on the text, click on Hyperlink, choose "Place in this Document" from the dialogue box, and click on "Top of the Document."

A Word About Graphics

I will be blunt here. The Kindle is not a lush graphic environment. The device has a 6-inch black-and-white screen and shows pictures with something like the resolution that one experienced with black-and-white newspaper photographs before the visually slick USA Today began to change newspaper production values. If you are the publisher of Architectural Digest or American Photo, this article is not for you.

That being said, I don't mean to imply that you have to publish a text-only edition of your magazine for Kindle. You can include artwork, as long as you are aware that it will be represented in black-and-white images of no more than about 6 inches by 4 inches. You can also make effective use of the opportunity that the Kindle platform offers to embed links in your content. By using links to graphic material effectively, you can provide your readers with the chance to view that material in a more suitable digital environment.

Another useful option is to provide a link to a website with all your graphics or an email link allowing readers to "opt in" to receive an email with a full set of visual links from each issue, so that they can be assured of being able to save and open those links on a desktop computer.

Uploading the Kindle Version of Your Zine

Publishing a Kindle edition of your magazine is both free and relatively easy, but as with everything else you do as a publisher, it is important to do things the right way from the start. Once you put your content out there on the Web, it is likely to remain out there permanently, even if you attempt to pull it back.

Getting things right for the Kindle applies, of course, to the usual processes of content preparation and your insistence on excellence. Equally important, however, are the initial processes of setting up your Kindle Edition in ways that will help you and Amazon to market your magazine effectively over the long haul. Items that need special care here include choosing a title and subtitle, selecting the content categories under which your title will be listed, writing a description of each issue, setting a retail price and establishing the search keywords under which each issue will be searchable in Amazon's Kindle inventory and, ultimately, elsewhere on the web as well.

Because these things are so critically important to your success as a Kindle publisher, it is essential that you prepare off-line for the process of following the steps presented here. Open a word processing file (or get out a yellow legal pad, if you prefer), and go through the publishing steps to prepare the content that you will use before you post it. This content will very likely be some of the most important marketing content you ever write for the Kindle edition of your magazine, so it is well worth a little extra time.

For specific navigation through the process of publishing your content for the Kindle platform, you will want to follow the steps delineated in Chapter II.2 on how to upload other books, articles, or other content for the Kindle, with the following further considerations:

Leave the ISBN field blank unless you use ISBNs (rather than ISSNs) for individual print issues of your periodical.

Enter the full title and subtitle (if any) of your magazine in the title field, with proper capitalization and a colon after the title. If your listing is for a "Lifetime Subscription" or "1997 Archive" or "Current Issue," include such labeling information prominently in the title line. You may even consider using all upper case for this info.

If your periodical has named special issues that help to distinguish the content of each issue, be sure to include these as subtitles.

Write a professional, attractive description of the specific issue that you are posting, with dense, copy aimed at inviting readers to read more and keywords that are likely to turn up in readers' likely searches. Don't exaggerate, embellish, or make false claims about the magazine, or disappointed readers will be sure to retaliate with negative reviews. Amazon will force you to be succinct, since the Description field is limited to 850 characters, or about 170 words.

In the "Publisher" field, consider taking a cue from *Inc.* magazine's "Inc.com" website and listing a shortened website address as the publisher name. You don't need the "http" or the slashes or even the "www" gobbledygook, but if you include the dot-com part of the address readers will recognize it as a web address and it can help drive traffic to your website.

Carefully select the Kindle content categories that Amazon will use to help readers find your content. Don't look for a "magazines" category, since you are posting under "Kindle Books." You will use "magazine" and the name of your journal under search keywords, in a moment. Category headings are different from keywords that you invent for your title. You are only allowed 5 categories, and they must all come from Amazon's tree structure of category and subcategory headings. When you see a plus sign next to a category, you can click to find subcategories. Study the choices and try to imagine the categories that your readers would be most likely to use if they were hunting for a book or article like yours. Don't try to trick the system, but do be open to spreading the field a bit by thinking about different types of appeal that your article might have. For instance, the keywords for this chapter, if it were a stand-along piece, might include "Marketing" as well as "Writing," two categories that appear in very different areas of the category key structure. If you have trouble finding the content category you are looking for, here's a tip: search for books that you think would be listed under that category until you find it, to see the route that the rather ornate Amazon category tree takes to arrive at the category in question.

Under "Authors," enter the names of as many as possible of your current issue's contributors, including authors, editors, illustrators, translators, etc. Although this may seem straightforward, one thing that is often overlooked is the importance of entering an author's name exactly as it may appear elsewhere in Amazon's catalogue. Since Amazon automatically hyperlinks author names, this consistency is essential if you want to make it easy for readers to find multiple works by the same author.

When it comes to keywords, don't get too arcane. Begin with keywords such as the name of your magazine and words such as "magazine," "journal," and "periodical." If this work-around catches on, Kindle owners will learn that they can use a search work-around of their own to find magazines.

Populate the fields for "Edition Number," "Series Title," and "Volume Number" with the standard bibliographic information. For instance, if this issue is Volume VII, Number 3, type VII:3 in the "Volume Number" field. "Edition Number" in this context is more germane to book and textbook editions, so you will probably want to leave it blank. For "Series Title," the name of the magazine itself (rather than any single issue) will do.

Upload an appropriate cover image in the "Product Image" field. A cover image of a hard-copy edition of your magazine is suitable here, and it can help to generate interest in your content just as covers attract browsers at newsstands or in bookstores. Your image must be in TIFF (.tif/.tiff) or JPEG (.jpg/.jpeg) format, and must be at least 500 pixels on the longest side. If you do not have a hard-copy edition of your book, it may be worthwhile to design and digitize a product image so that you can upload it here to enhance the browsing experience. It is not strictly necessary, however, and you may also add an image at any time after you have published your content as a Kindle edition. Changing the cover image with each new issue will help to provide readers and browsers with a heads up about new content. Including that cover image in your update notification email is a nice branding touch.

Making Optimal Use
Of the Kindle DTP's Marketing Power

Lurking somewhere behind Ben's equation of cost vs. circulation, of course, there is always that central question of commercial or cultural reach: once you have produced them, how do you sell them? How do you get people to want them, or even to know they are there? Any way you phrase it, it comes down, if I may be permitted to mangle James Carville's famous line, to "It's the marketing, stupid!"

By keeping a tight lid on the number of magazine and newspaper subscriptions available to Kindle readers in the initial months since the Kindle's launch, Amazon has provided a valuable leg up for its three dozen or so anointed periodicals. Several of these publications sit at or near the top of the overall Kindle Store list of top sellers, and in Amazon's store good sales almost invariably lead to better sales because of the way they place a title before a growing number of eyeballs. One even wonders if the desire to create this somewhat tilted playing field may have been central to Amazon's purpose in limiting early access for the newspaper and magazine crowd. But let's not wallow in conspiracy theories; the fact is that any newspaper, magazine, book or other document can climb the list of Kindle top sellers and achieve a respectable position there if it is distinguished both by its quality and by having a potential market niche that significantly overlaps, somewhere and somehow, with the growing population of Kindle owners.

The Kindle DTP makes it fairly easy for publishers and authors who know what they are doing (because they have read this article, or were simply a lot smarter than me to begin with) to upload and optimize their content and listing details with the kind of powerful keywords that attract readers. The processes of using the Kindle, like the processes of using the main Amazon website, tend to train people into becoming good searchers for the kind of content that they like to read.

You shouldn't compose your search keyword lists on the Amazon screens any more than you should write a novel on the

Amazon screens. In addition to the fact that drafting this material off-line will allow you to edit, revise and improve it, it also carries the extra benefit of allowing you to save the material in document form so that you can use it again or get it back if you somehow lose your Internet connection or your place in the process midstream.

Always make effective use of catalog category and keyword fields on each detail page to draw traffic. For an example of what I mean here, let's take a look at a back issue of *Ploughshares*, a venerable Boston-area literary magazine, from the winter of 1995-1996, which you can find in Amazon's catalog   at http://www.amazon.com/exec/obidos/ASIN/0933277156/ebest.

Although this is a paper or hard-copy listing, the same basic approach applies. The detail page for the listing is dense with information, with the date of the issue, the "stories and poems" subheading, the hyperlinked names of issue editors Tim O'Brien and Mark Strand, and a "product description" that lists the full names of over 40 contributors to this issue. While it is great to list this information, it would be even better if the page were search-optimized, with the contributors' names included as searchable keywords or tags or, if space allowed, as names included in the subtitle or author listings. Then this issue of *Ploughshares* would come up in a reader's search if, for instance, the reader were to type in the name of the poet Judith Berke, just as it comes up if one types in the name of O'Brien or Strand.

Once your title is live, I encourage you to buy a "copy" yourself if you own a Kindle. In addition to priming the sales pump, it will also provide you with the only certain way to check your content and formatting exactly as it will appear to all your other readers. Once you purchase a Kindle title, Amazon will allow you to download or refresh it again as many times as you want, which will also allow you to check for updated content that you may upload in the future. You will then be able, for instance, to confirm that your content has been has been updated before you send out an email notifying your subscribers that new content or a new issue is available for free download. To save yourself a few dollars, you might want to make this purchase while your title is still in a 99-cent beta state. As with all your readers or customers, the relationship between what you paid for a title and a price that may be set for it later should never matter – if you buy it once, you should be able to download it forever in its most recent state.

Approaches to Presenting a Newspaper
In the Kindle Store

If such a work-around approach can work for magazines, might it also work for a newspaper? Not exactly, is my short answer. The two primary obstacles are obvious:

* The current turnaround time of 12 to 72 hours between content upload and Kindle Store availability would sap the currency of a daily newspaper and make it a poor competitor with other newspapers that are available, and pushed to subscribers' Kindles, before dawn.

* The glut of daily "title" iterations that would be necessary to represent a daily newspaper's presence in the Kindle Store using such a work-around approach would clutter the Kindle Store inelegantly and create confusion and annoyance for readers, browsers and content searchers.

That being said, the work-around model suggested here could support a couple of approaches that might be worthy of consideration for a newspaper's digital content department:

* a weekly digital for format presenting the best, most emailed, and, perhaps, most timeless and readable pieces from each week's newspaper; and

* an archiving service that would make powerful use of the Kindle's support for hyperlinked Index and Table of Contents features as well as other internal and external linking.

With each of these approaches, every article could be punctuated with links to the appropriate subject areas of the newspaper's digital content site and daily only edition. Ideally, such a Kindle edition "weekly digest" or archive would provide

* a nice reading experience;

* content whose currency might make it an effective search and traffic magnet;

* an engine to promote traffic from the Kindle edition to the newspaper's primary digital site;

* a revenue source through sales; and

* an additional revenue source, where appropriate, through embedded advertising and Amazon Associates product links.

The archiving feature could be updated with new content at the end of each week, and also packaged for sale on a monthly, quarterly or annual basis.

Chapter II.5

Start Earning a Living Today Writing Articles for the Kindle

Thinking Outside the Box as a Writer

Journalists, free-lance writers, copywriters and authors! Throw off your chains!

Have you had it up to here with the query-and-submission rat race of submitting magazine pieces, the exploitation of web-content copywriting websites that pay you on a dimes-to-dollars basis for the deadline drudgework that makes thousands of dollars in web traffic revenue for them, or the lethally boring day job that is supposed to be supporting your writing dreams?

You may be closer than you think to the point where you can be paid well and fairly for writing about topics that interest you. When Jeff Bezos and his Amazonians launched the Kindle "e-book reader" in November 2007, they weren't only trying to line their own pockets. They were trying to line yours, too.

Don't believe it? Read on.

You don't need to write the next Great American Novel, or even a celebrity bio or Oprah-licious self-help book, to find writing success on the Amazon Kindle publishing platform.

It is so easy to waste precious time thinking inside the box as a writer. The literary-industrial complex conditions us rather thoroughly to accept its structure and its gatekeepers.

Writing a book? Find an agent or a publisher!

Have a good idea for an article? Submit a query! Then submit the article to magazines!

Having trouble getting published? Keep your head down and keep plugging! We only publish the very best 1 per cent, or 1/10 of 1 per cent, or whatever we feel like telling you today!

Still not getting published? Get an MFA! Attend a workshop! Enter your work in a contest! (Make your check payable to….)

Need to pay the rent? Go to work as a copywriter for one of those web content outfits!

Well, uh … *Not!*

You can manage your own writing career and make it pay by writing material that people want or need to read and publishing it on the Amazon Kindle Digital Text Platform. Write well, make it relevant to the interests of a significant niche of readers, and optimize it for search, and you will be amazed at the satisfaction and rewards your work can bring.

You do not have to be a techno-geek to succeed at this. You do not have to own a Kindle.

You do have to know what you are talking about, either because you know it already or because you do the required research. It would also help a great deal if you are able to write clearly and concisely.

Skipping the Middleman:
Why the Kindle Is Ideal for Short Pieces

The Kindle provides an ideal platform for "short-form" publishing including articles, essays, short stories and reports. You can even excerpt appropriate chapters from a longer work in progress.

What makes the Kindle so great for shorter content?

1. The Kindle is a highly evolved search-and-read environment that exists for the primary purpose of connecting readers with the content that they seek. If you can provide that content, you rule.

2. While the Kindle is certainly a fine medium for reading *War and Peace*, for many owners it is even better for reading shorter material. An article or two can pass the time and edify a reader on the train or the plane, at the doctor's office or over a reader's morning coffee. Kindle readers are curious and inquisitive people almost by definition, and it is up to you as a writer to satisfy their curiosities.

3. With the Kindle, there is no middleman, broker, or editor to get in between you and your readers. If you write it, they will come. You could think of the Amazon Kindle store as the entity that is playing that brokering, middle-man role, but once you learn how to make optimal use of the Amazon environment you will come to see it as something that is there to help you connect with readers.

Warning: This lack of a middleman can be a great thing, but the naked relationship between you and your readers can also be rife with danger. Unless you are working with an editor or other professional support staff, the burden is entirely on you to polish, package and present your work on the Kindle platform. Good editing and proofreading is essential, and the time that you devote to these activities as well as the presentation of your bibliographic and search material on the Digital Text Platform will directly influence the success of your titles.

Brainstorming and Selecting the Right Content

Many talented writers are generalists who don't necessarily think of themselves as experts on much of anything other than Coleridge, Hemingway, and how to write a pretty good sentence or paragraph. If you have every felt a pang of identification with Garrison Keillor's witty radio parodies aimed at the career dreams and lamentations of English majors, you may not feel prepared to assert your capacity to write expert articles on topics that writers are likely to search out, buy, and download them on their Kindles. I'm not here to convince you otherwise if you are certain you are a know-nothing with negligible research skills. However, I do recommend that you explore the universe of interesting and useful topics about which you may surprise yourself with your ability to present the information people need or want to absorb.

My suggestion is that you begin by sitting down with a legal pad and your computer to do some brainstorming. Depending on the architecture of your brain, you may come up with some much more elegant way of organizing this process, but when I have done this kind of brainstorming I have found it useful to make 5 columns: a wide column on the left for possible topics, aligned with four more narrow columns at the right for checkmarks, brief comments, or numerical ratings. For each topic, the columns at the right will allow you to enter some sort of meaningful rating on each of these questions:

What is your current level of expertise?

What is the potential, based on the availability of information and your ability to focus on and make sense of that information, for you to attain an appropriate level of expertise through research.

What is your level of interest and passion for this topic? Assuming that you have a reasonable range of interests, life is too short for you to bore yourself silly writing about subject matter that does not interest you?

How "hot" or topical or otherwise important to people is the topic in question at the present time. In most cases, you are not looking for thin, broad interest. You will generally do best if you can identify niche groups of people whose interest is more intense – they *need* to know – in very specific subject matter.

It may help you to achieve the proper, positive brainstorming approach if you try to imagine yourself as the author of a series of articles, pamphlets, booklets, or books: *The*

One-Minute Blanker, How to Blank in Thirty Days Or Less, Blanking for Dummies, Blanking Hacks, The Complete Idiot's Guide to Blanking, etc.

I did this with an imaginary series under the working series title, ***Ten Weeks to a Better Blank, Ten Weeks to Better Blank-Making***, etc. I made a point of believing in my capacity to write usefully and clearly about as many of the possibilities that came to mind as I could. I did not reject any topics out of hand unless the thought of having to write about them made my hair hurt.

Now I will admit that I have a wide range of interests, and a naturally inquisitive mind. I am a bit of a polymath, and the combination of my experiences in journalism, politics, and organizing allow me to address a wide variety of topics with the appearance, at least, of authority. After less than two hours I had come up with a list of 200 topics that would fit nicely into a ***Ten Weeks*** series. If I can come up with 200 article topics in two hours, I'm sure you can come up with your own very good list with one hand tied behind your back.

It may also well be that you are working with a much higher order of knowledge, teachable skills, and information than my fairly generalist base of knowledge. If so, if you are highly knowledgeable about one or more area of technology, science, personal finance, college admissions, or child nutrition, for instance, you are already way ahead of the rest of us. Your ability to turn a topic into marketable writing depends mainly upon your ability to determine what it is specifically about the topic that people want to know, who the people are that want to know it, how to organize the information into a manageable written package, and how to connect with these people in acceptable ways to make them aware that the knowledge and answers that they want are now available.

There are countless ways in which you can research what topics are hot, but the Amazon bestseller list, organizing by nonfiction categories, and the various searchable lists of most frequently searched and emailed articles and topics on Google, Google News, and elsewhere are good places to start. Not to put too fine a point on a notion that could be construed by some as the base suggestion that you write about to the market, but the steps that you will go throw below in optimizing your articles for search will also point you in helpful directions for selecting and zeroing in on topics that will engage readers.

When considering nonfiction article topics, focus on pieces that explain how to do things or make personal changes that are important to people. The top items on such a list are straightforward and rather timeless:

* make money

* save money

* lose weight

* achieve greater fitness

* increase one's sex appeal

* raise happy, obedient, successful children

Don't base your content on your opinions. You are entitled to your opinions, but few people are likely to pay you to read them.

Hone in on your areas of expertise and interest. Writers usually do their best work when they write what they know, what they are passionate about, or both. If there are topics that interest you where your knowledge is not totally current and comprehensive, can you fill in the gaps with some thorough research?

Research and develop possible topics and subject matter for articles by reviewing the websites of popular content providers, including the Amazon.com catalog and websites such as *about.com, wikihow* and *ehow.com*. Spend a couple of hours at your local public library checking out the content in popular magazines, particularly those in the fields of your own expertise. Explore the nonfiction bestseller lists, particularly those on Amazon and in the Kindle Store. Take notes and pay particular attention, as you go, to the categories, search words, titles, subtitles and descriptions of the most popular content.

If you are working on a book or other long nonfiction project, consider excerpting chapters where they could appropriately stand alone as articles on the Kindle publishing platform. This approach can provide an excellent way to market-test your book as you work on the project, while it also provides some month-to-month income while you work. Go over your outline or projected Table of Contents to mine potential short-form article topics. Tailor the titles of such excerpted articles to the need to present them properly in the Kindle catalog rather than to the less defined needs of a book's Table of Contents or chapter headings.

Optimize for Search: Helping Readers Find Your Content

Define the market for your article (or articles) before you get down to work. You should be able to identify specific groups of people who are most likely to be interested in purchasing and reading your content. For example, this article is most likely to appeal to journalists, free-lance writers, copywriters and other writers who may want to try their hands at short-form publishing.

Think specifically about how your readers will find your content. What are the keywords that they are most likely to use to search the kind of content you are posting? Begin by making a list of your own, then use a tool like the Google Adwords Keyword Tool at https://adwords.google.com/select/KeywordToolExternal to branch out and experiment with variations and subtopics. In the process, be on the lookout for spin-off topics for future writing projects. Build your best keywords into your title, your content, and the description and keywords list that you post on the Digital Text Platform.

This practice of sprinkling the right keywords properly throughout your content, title, description and "meta tags" will soon become second nature to you as a writer, if it hasn't already. Keywords are critical if you want readers to be able to find your content, and they can ultimately drive traffic to your titles not only within the Amazon and Kindle environments but also beyond Amazon with search engines such as Google and Yahoo. There is a delicate balance between liberal keyword sprinkling, which is a good thing, and ridiculously overdoing it, which will defeat the quality of your content, drive readers away, and often cause search engines to ignore or penalize you.

Emphasize Quality

Naturally, the quality of your content is every bit as important as the help that you provide to readers in their efforts to find it. If the titles that you make available for readers to purchase in the Kindle Store are not up to snuff, the "wisdom of crowds" -- in the form of negative or mediocre customer reviews and tags -- will turn traffic away from your titles. Quality means different things to different people, of course, but with nonfiction pieces that readers are selecting for information and self-education, the critical elements of quality are clear, concise writing and pertinence. If you post an article whose descriptive material claims that it will save readers thousands on their income taxes, and the only point of the article is to say that you can reduce your income taxes by reducing your income, your piece will probably get tagged and reviewed as a scam, and readers will stay away. The fact that this experience may make you a poster child for your own article by reducing your income will be cold comfort.

Linking to Revenue

If you plan to publish and sell nonfiction content on the Amazon Kindle website, it behooves you to establish a supplemental income stream by setting up an Amazon Associates account. Whenever you link to a book or other product at Amazon and a reader uses that link (equipped with your Amazon Associates customer code) to navigate to and purchase the product from Amazon, you will be paid between 4% and 10% of the retail price for your referral. It costs you nothing to participate, and you can include such links in the content that you publish for the Kindle as well as on any web pages that you use to promote your titles or otherwise provide information for your readers.

Are your readers likely to be offended to find such links in the articles or other content that you post in the Kindle store? Au contraire. Hyperlinks that help them to navigate to other worthwhile content will enrich their reading experience and help them to get the most out of the Kindle experience. Naturally, if you post "articles" that are little more than link lists in hopes of harvesting affiliate program revenue, your material will be recognized for what it is and tagged or reviewed as such, with the predictable effect on readership, traffic, sales and, of course, affiliate fees. By the same token, if you make a regular habit of including links to other content that is lacking in quality, your own credibility as an author and authority will be greatly diminished.

One caveat regarding embedded links, and a suggestion for overcoming the potential problem:

The ability to navigate to external web pages from links embedded in Kindle content is both a helpful feature when used sparingly and a drain on a Kindle's system resources. The more graphical and complex a website, the slower it will be to load on the Kindle and the greater the chance it will "freeze" the device's screen, or processor, which will require the Kindle owner to use the tiny "reset" pinhole beneath the Kindle's back cover and, probably, to clear the web browser's cache from the Basic Web settings page.

If your article includes a lot of links, invite your readers to email a "code" to you in order to receive the content as a Word attachment so that they can use the links directly from their personal computers.

Connecting to Your Kindle Titles
From a Blog or Website

Build clean, logical connections between the articles or other work that you post and the websites, blogs or web pages that you use to present and promote your work. Don't overdo it by including links to your website on every page or in every paragraph, but it is fine to include a link or two in your content, and perhaps even to use a web address as your "publisher name" when you post your material on the Kindle Digital Text Platform, so that the URL will show up prominently on your titles' product detail pages.

Maintaining the Currency of Your Articles

Keep your articles current and they could continue to sell for years. It is easy to update any Kindle title and re-publish it without missing a beat. Once a reader buys your article, he can come back any time and refresh the content at no charge by downloading the most recent version of that article (as identified by its 10-digit ASIN) that you have published. In order to allow readers to take advantage of this feature, you may want include a notice prominently positioned in each article that you write that readers may "register" with you via e-mail if they want to receive notification of future updates. Naturally, if you are going to offer this feature, it is important that you follow through on the offer.

Pricing

The general pricing market for digital content in the Kindle Store is $9.99 for bestsellers and books that are otherwise available in hardcover, $2.99 to $6.99 for books that are otherwise available in paperback, and $0.99 to $2.99 for articles, short stories, and other short-form content. You will be paid 35% of the retail price for any document that is sold in the Kindle Store on your behalf, which means that you will net 35 cents for an article that sells for 99 cents, 87 cents for an article that sells for $2.49, and $1.05 for an article that sells for $2.99.

However, it is worth noting that the Kindle Store frequently applies a 20% discount to the retail list price that you set for a title. This discount does not lower the amount that you will be paid, but since it lowers the purchase price for your customer, you may want to experiment with a high retail list price in order to increase the royalty that you will receive. For instance, if you want your potential customers to pay $1.99 for an article that you are making available, try setting the retail list price at $2.49. If Amazon applies its 20% discount, your customers will pay $1.99, but the 87-cent royalty that you will receive based on 35% of the $2.49 retail list price will amount to 44% of the price you intended for the title.

Obviously, at royalty levels such as these, it takes a while to begin earning significant income. But here are a few things to keep in mind:

* The key to success in building up an income publishing your content for the Kindle platform is to keep writing, to keep publishing, and to build a larger and larger catalog of quality pieces. Maintain their currency by updating them regularly. If you write at least one article a week you'll have 50 pieces earning writing revenue for you at the end of a year. If you build during the course of that year to an average of 5 copies a day sold for each piece at a retail price of $2.49, you'll have reached the point where you are earning over $75,000 per year with your writing.

* If you doubt your ability to average 5 copies a day per article, consider this. The number of Kindles in circulation is growing every week. A conservative estimate says that there will be 5 to 10 times as many Kindles in circulation a year from now as there are today. If you can sell a copy a day of an article

today, you have a very good chance of selling 5 copies a day a year from now, unless it becomes outdated, just based on the growth of the readership market. The first chapter that I excerpted from this book-in-progress, "20 Steps to Publishing a Kindle Edition of Your Book or Document," was published as a Kindle article on December 1, 2007. It sold 9 copies in the first half of December, 24 copies in the second half of December, 98 copies in January, and 136 copies in February. My piece on how to use the Kindle for email and other tricks sold 3 copies in December, 1299 in January, 1925 in February, 1487 in March when no new Kindles were shipped, and 4043 in April. Other pieces have followed a similar pattern of growth, at whatever level they established.

It is unlikely, of course, that there would be an even spread of sales performance among your various titles if you post a dozen titles on the Kindle or on any other retail channel. More likely, in keeping with the basic principles of long-tail economics, out of a dozen titles, half a dozen might sell slowly, a handful might experience moderate sales, and one or two might stand a chance of becoming hits. There is a good change you will know what the hits will be, based on your subject matter and title, before you write them. The hits are extremely valuable, not only because of the royalties you earn from them directly, but because as they climb the sales ladder they will secure better and better real estate on the Amazon and Kindle websites, which in turn will boost their sales even farther and, as readers and browsers see what else shows up (through Amazon's highly associative product placement process), they can also boost the sales of your other titles. It does not work with Reaganomics, but in Amazonomics, a rising tide will often lift all boats.

A Few Final Tips

* Use proper documentation, attribution and citations when you are referring to material from other sources. Never plagiarize another writer's work. Familiarize yourself with

copyright law and fair use doctrine. Where appropriate, use hyperlinks instead of footnotes.

* Conduct yourself as a professional author. Please don't be offended, because I am certainly not addressing *you* here in any specific sense. However, since anyone can publish material on the Kindle platform, it's worth saying once here to that other guy, the vulgarian who crashed our party. The Amazon bookstore is not a hobby site or anyone's personal blog, and this is as true of the Kindle store as it is of the "main bookstore." Conduct thorough professional research and interview helpful sources in the course of preparing expert articles.

* Market yourself as a content writer and producer. Print a business card and carry it with you, with the URL of your website where a reader can find links to all your books, articles, stories or content of any kind. A few sales of a given title can make a big difference in your sales ranking and consequently in your future sales.

* Track your sales, set goals, and measure results. It can be great fun to watch your titles ascend the Amazon Sales Rankings in the main store or in the Kindle store, and some writers even find it a bit addictive! Be careful -- don't spend so much time watching one article's sales rankings that you never write another!

- 118 -

Chapter II.6

The Business Side of Publishing
On the Kindle Platform

"Publication," wrote Emily Dickinson, "is the Auction of the Mind." She tied her poems in bundles, and put them in a drawer.

She didn't have access, of course, to the Kindle publishing platform.

For those of us who see our writing as our livelihood, it is likely that we have already come to grips with the fact that we must do a little auctioneering, in one form or another. The Kindle provides writers with the opportunity to attend to this entrepreneurial, business side of our writing lives in a straightforward, dignified, and potentially lucrative manner. It need not and probably should not be the only opportunity of which we avail ourselves, but it is a good start and can even help us to approach other opportunities in a rational and well-informed way.

In this chapter I will try to provide a few tips and tactics to help you navigate the business side of life as a Kindle author. Naturally, the first thing worth pointing out about the Kindle platform is that an author does not have to focus on any business considerations – beyond having an Amazon account and a U.S. bank account and agreeing to the standard Kindle agreement -- to publish there. Since there are no associated costs for production, warehousing or fulfillment, anyone can feel free to make his own content available with absolutely no thought for profit margins, cost of goods sold, or, for that matter, sales.

Perhaps that is how Ms. Dickinson would have approached it (although I seriously doubt it).

But if it is worth publishing your content, it must also be worth connecting with readers, and that implies sales. And, not to put too fine a point on it, business.

Tracking Sales

Naturally, you will want to keep track of the sales of the titles that you make available on the Kindle's Digital Text Platform. Knowing how you are doing in sales can help to provide you with valuable feedback as an author-publisher on key questions such as:

* Which future projects make the most economic sense?

* Which Kindle edition titles should be brought out in print-on-paper editions?

* What additional steps should you take to market your titles?

* Should you submit a title to a traditional publisher, backed up by your Kindle sales figures?

There are three easy ways to keep tabs on your Kindle sales and sales rankings:

* The "My Reports" page on the Kindle's Digital Text Platform allows you to look at sales for any date range you choose. These reports usually update about in something close to real time, although there is occasionally a lag. The bulk of sales occur between 10 a.m. and midnight Eastern time.

* It is easy to add your titles to your Amazon author profile page. Once you have published several titles for the Kindle or anywhere else in the Amazon store, it becomes much more efficient to use your Amazon author profile page's "bibliography" section to follow your sales. When your titles are added to your author bibliography, Amazon will automatically include your Amazon sales rankings for each title. Take a look

at my Author profile page. Scroll down past the blog entries and you will get an idea about how much time it saves me to have Amazon keep tabs on all my sales rankings on one easy-to-find page.

* The sweetest sales report, of course, is the one that tells you what you will get paid. Just navigate to the same "My Reports" page on the Kindle's Digital Text Platform, and select "Settlements" instead of "Transactions." You will see a date range once a monthly payment period has been closed out. Scroll down to the "Net Balance" to see how much Amazon owes you for that period, based on the 35% royalty that it pays for Kindle titles.

Concerning sales rankings, it is important to keep in mind that there are now only about 120,000 titles in the Kindle store, as compared with over 6 million titles in the main Amazon store. Consequently, a sales ranking of 1,000 in the Kindle store is attainable with fewer than five sales per day, and corresponds roughly to a sales ranking of about 50,000 in the main Amazon store. Half a dozen sales per day would take a title into the top 500 among Kindle books, and over 100 sales per day would place a Kindle title in the top 10. Naturally, as the number of Kindle titles and Kindle owners continues to grow, it will take greater and greater sales to attain these sales ranking levels.

Watching actual sales "synch up" with your titles' sales rankings can be a little frustrating, because there is often a delay on one side or the other, but my experience has been that they always catch up eventually. Amazon has been paying my publishing company for hardcopies since 2001 and they have never shorted us, so I am optimistic that we will be paid in full. I have also noticed the phenomenon of a title moving up the rankings with no sales registered in the "Reports" tally. At one point in January 2008 my novel Say My Name jumped from oblivion to the 11,000 range, and the next day to 853, but it took another ten days for anything to appear in the "Reports" tally. One possible explanation, and it is just a shot in the dark, may be a distinction between "orders" and "shipments." if the sales rankings are registering order of Kindle titles by customers before their Kindle units have shipped. Meanwhile, let me say that patience seems to bear fruit here in the happy confluence of several factors including the growth in number of Kindle units in circulation and the myriad ways in which the Kindle and Amazon environments help sell whatever is selling.

Payment of Royalties

Amazon is currently paying a straight royalty of 35% of retail list price for Kindle titles. If you are the author-publisher, you will receive all of this royalty. If your title is under the control of a publisher other than you, the breakdown of this royalty is subject to the agreements between you and your publisher. Naturally, if you are a publisher handling the content for authors whose rights you control, it is incumbent upon you to pay the author's share of his royalty directly to the author out of the funds you receive from Amazon for Kindle edition sales.

Amazon will pay you your Kindle royalties about 60 to 90 days after your sales occur. To be more precise, using the month of January as an example, your royalties for January should be deposited in your account by early April. Kindle royalties are always paid by ACH electronic deposit into your checking account, and it is up to you to provide and maintain the accuracy of your account information on the "My Accounts" page.

Pricing of Your Amazon Kindle Titles

With Amazon leading the way by setting $9.99 as the default price for bestsellers otherwise available only in hardcover, a general pricing scheme emerged quickly for Kindle titles: $9.99 for titles otherwise available only in hardcover, $5.99 to 7.99 for trade paperbacks, $3.19 to $4.99 for titles available as mass-market paperbacks, and $0.99 to $2.99 for short-form articles, stories, and other content.

However, authors and publishers should not hesitate to set higher prices for content whose print-version prices are justifiably higher than the norm. In general, buyers are more likely to pay a premium for highly technical content, for something that will have a direct impact on their pocketbooks, or for content that may involve multiple contributors, graphics, or the need to pay royalties to several contributors. In some cases, the fact that the only other extant edition is a paperback is less important, if it was a paperback original at a reasonably high price point. You should also be prepared to set a higher price if special expenses demand it, such as royalties that you may have to pay to contributors.

One thing that has been working for a number of publishers and authors in the initial post-launch phase, with regard to setting prices for a Kindle edition, is to bring the price down into a lower range in order to build a sales track record. We have had very good success with some short-form publishing of article-length book excerpts with an initial price in the $0.99 to $2.49 range, with several titles that have jumped around in the top 500 or so. When any title comes up at the top of its category sales rankings, it is likely to generate a lot more sales traffic. Unlike the Amazon Advantage platform, there is no apparent resistance on the DTP to authors or publishers deciding to change prices from time to time.

For a paperback original that you are offering for the first time on the Kindle platform, the market price range probably runs from $5.99 to $7.99. But it might not be the worst idea in the world to ratchet down the price for a while at the start in order to allow some "impulse" buying of the Kindle edition, which would bump you up the sales ranking ladders and might help you sell more copies at higher prices in the future. You've got nothing to lose but your production costs, in my view, and those production costs total out at $0.00.

If the number of Kindles in circulation grows steadily throughout 2008 so that a year from now it is a significant multiple times the current number, then the price you are getting in the fourth quarter 2008 is likely to be more important than the need to get a good price now. It will be interesting to see how all of this plays out.

It's easy to change the price of one of your Kindle titles. Just go into the "My Shelf" area of the Kindle's Digital Text Platform. Click on the title whose price you wish to modify, select "Enter Price," and change the price in the Price field. Then click on "Save Entries" and on "Publish," in that order. It usually takes about 12 hours for such information to update in the Kindle system, and during that time you will not be able to make any changes applicable to the title in question. The only downside of making a change in price is that, during these initial hours, a prospective buyer may see one price on the title's detail page and the new price on the transaction page. Given the potential for such a change to lead to disgruntled buyers, my personal preference for the best time to make a price change is at about 11 p.m., so as to minimize any "in progress" impact.

If you notice that Amazon unilaterally reduces the price that you set for a title, don't worry. Amazon frequently discounts the list price of titles either in its Kindle Store or in its main store, as a promotional strategy. Such a discount does not reduce the royalties that you will be paid, since these royalties are based on 35% of the list price for any item. Indeed, if Amazon lowers the price of your title, you will probably make even more money than you otherwise would make from sales of that title, since lower prices usually boost sales.

Projecting a Kindle Future

It is probably obvious to you already that I am keenly interested, as an author, in the commerce, technology, and business of publishing reading material of all kinds. Frankly, I have difficulty understanding how any writer can fail to be interested in these matters, because they bear so heavily on the ways in which we can connect with readers and the economics of the writing life for all of us, from those who are doing fabulously well to those for whom the struggle to keep the wolf from the door is constant. In any case, if you are thinking about publishing your work for the Kindle, I strongly recommend that you find out as much as you can about what this device. I say this not to shill for the writing I do about the Kindle as a gadget (see -- there's no link here!). A good place to start is to navigate to the video of Charlie Rose interviewing Jeff Bezos about the Kindle on Amazon's main Kindle page. It's worth spending the 54 minutes because it is worth knowing the extent of Bezos' commitment to this product from the first day of its launch, and to understand that his personal vision for the Kindle is explicitly inclusive of some of the kinds of author experimentation contemplated in this book. He speaks unabashedly about his belief that the Kindle eventually will allow readers to access every book ever written. It is equally clear that he expects, eventually, for a very large percentage of serious readers to own Kindles.

Of course, it is easy to say that Bezos is just trying to line his pockets by playing cheerleader for the Kindle. Personally what I see is more significant than that. Here's a guy whose net worth is $9 billion putting all of his credibility behind his claims and hopes for a revolutionary product. It is a product in an industry where his company is the single most influential player. It does not cinch the Kindle's success, but it persuades me to listen carefully to his efforts to express his vision for this product.

Some of the dialogue between Bezos and Rose seemed like the big tease:

Rose: "Why the name, 'Kindle?'"

Bezos: "To start a fire. "

R: "In your mind, your imagination, wherever?"

B: "Absolutely."

R: "To start a fire, to create a revolution in the world of books?"

B: "Absolutely."

What is remarkable, for now, is how little we know, numbers wise, about the Kindle. I had hoped that Amazon would share some information, when it released its quarterly 10-Q financial reports on January 30, 2008, concerning how many

Kindles were sold and produced during the fourth quarter of 2007. Not a peep, outside of his statement that he was "super-excited" at demand for the Kindle. I have seen no disclosures and very little in the way of useful estimates on this question, which is important to me as a Kindle author. At best, when I wrote my first draft of this chapter in mid-February 2008, I was able to extrapolate a very conservative estimate of 20,000-plus "Kindles in circulation" based on the following:

* Of several titles I have offered for sale in Kindle editions, one title had sold 2,079 Kindle copies since it became available in late December, and it had averaged about 100 copies a day from January 23 to mid-February. This had been enough to place the title in the top 5 to 7 Kindle titles for a few weeks.

* It was my educated but unscientific guess that it was extremely unlikely that more than 1 out of 10 Kindle owners had downloaded this title, so I concluded crudely that there were at least 20,790 Kindles in circulation, and that Amazon had been shipping 500 to 1000 a day, on average. I believed at that point that these guesses were conservative, and that the real number was north of 40,000. But it was all just extrapolation and guesswork.

The April Amazon conference call came and went without any more guidance from the company about the number of Kindles in circulation, but a few days later somebody finally sang. The CEO of Taiwan-based Prime View International announced that it had been supplying Amazon and Sony with 60,000 to 80,000 e-reader display screens per month, and that about 60% of the total had been shipping to Amazon for the Kindle. Based on five months of history at the time, this suggested that there might be 180,000 to 240,000 Kindles in circulation as of May 1, a number higher than most estimates that had been made at that point.

Another way of looking at this metric is that of the 40 million unique individuals who visit Amazon's website, 0.45% had purchased the single product most prominently displayed on that website for the previous six months. Seen that way,

180,000, 180,000 Kindles after 6 months does not seem like so many.

Even more stunning was a forward-looking statement made by the CEO if publicly traded PVI in the same announcement that PVI's production of e-reader display screen would ramp up to 140,000 per month by the end of 2008.

Assuming a very gradual ramp-up rate of 10,000 units per month, and allowing for gradual growth of Sony's production as part of the overall PVI order growth, any reasonable extrapolation from the PVI projections suggests that the number of Kindles in circulation would grow by 300 to 400 per cent from May 1 to the end of 2008, or perhaps allowing for a slower-than-likely manufacturing and fulfillment process, to the end of the first quarter of 2009. Without any regard for seasonality, I came up with this crude model for Kindle growth:

May 1, 2008 – 180,000 to 240,000 Kindles in circulation

May: 48,000 new Kindles

June: 54,000 to 56,000 new Kindles

July: 60,000 to 64,000 new Kindles

August: 66,000 to 72,000 new Kindles

September: 72,000 to 80,000 new Kindles

October: 78,000 to 88,000 new Kindles

November: 84,000 to 96,000 new Kindles

December: 84,000 to 96,000 new Kindles

Total number of Kindles in circulation by late 2008 or early 2009: 726,000 to 838,000.

If you have a title that is selling 50 copies a month as of today, it is reasonable to speculate that you have a good chance of doubling that figure by September and tripling it by early 2009. I don't want to attempt to put too fine a point on such speculative extrapolations, but I will say this. A big part of the beauty and excitement that authors and publishers should now be feeling about the Kindle is based upon the fact that its ownership base will continue to grow steadily and will continue to be composed, by definition, of motivated readers.

Naturally, there are downside forces too. As I write this chapter there are just over 120,000 titles available for the Kindle. It is very clear from the Bezos interview that he expects that figures to grow steadily, with the result that Kindle owners will have more and more choices in addition to your titles. But competition between titles does not necessarily mean declining sales. As the Kindle Store's selection grows, the number of Kindle customers is almost certain, at the very least, to keep pace.

You will need a well-planned long-term marketing strategy to continue to get reader attention for your titles as the Kindle catalog grows. You will also need to keep writing fresh, quality material and to do a good job of inter-linking all your titles.

What do I mean by "inter-linking all your titles"? Well, this may be a case of asking you to do what I say and not what I do, because I have some catching up to do here, but take a look at this review posted by our publishing company, Harvard Perspectives Press, for one of our articles. As you can see, each time an Amazon visitors navigates to the page for my article, "How to Use the Amazon Kindle for Email & Other Cool Tricks," they will see links to several other titles. Using such links in reviews, AmazonConnect blog entries and Listmania entries is a great way to take advantage of your placement in Amazon's virtual real estate to secure more sales. Hopefully, Amazon will soon make it possible for authors and publishers to post more substantial, linked content in our editorial and descriptive material about our books, so that we will not have to use the work-around device of posting "customer" reviews.

But it is clear that the Kindle platform is an important place to be, where e-books and digital publishing are concerned. Publishers will scramble to be included in the Kindle growth market. Kindle sales will grow dramatically, but they will remain just a tiny fraction of the book market. As they climb from, say, 2% at year-end 2008 to 5% or more by year-end

2009, they will begin to have an impact on the overall sales, marketing and production strategies of the book trade.

There's no way of getting around the fact that, implicitly on every page of this book, I am encouraging the emerging writer to be a cowboy, to be a cowgirl, to go for it: You Go, Boy! That can be a wonderful experience, but it can also, depending upon your personality, be dangerous. You are entering an arena of business and creative activity which will tend to compound what is probably your pre-existing propensity to work alone, to depend upon yourself, and to be confident in your ability to do things yourself rather than to delegate them to others. William H. Gass, D.H. Lawrence, and others have remarked with exhilaration upon the novelist's special placement as Deity in the created world of a novel, and when the Author is also the Publisher there can be little doubt that she will experience a similarly bracing, if sometimes daunting, sense of omnipotence. No need to walk on eggshells: You are In Charge!

Well, Whoa.

Get as much as you can in terms of focus, and motivation from your placement at the top of your organizational chart, but also recognize that there is a difference between Omnipotence and Competence. Recognize what you do well and what you don't know how to do, and get help. Don't be afraid of making an occasional mistake, but protect yourself from making too big a mistake by identifying the resources you need to complement your creative energy with a thorough, highly competent attention to detail.

Plenty of creative people stop right there, daunted. "I'm not going to spend two or three years getting an MBA just so I can publish a book," they may say.

But a better solution for finding the delicate balance between creative energy and business competence may be in getting help that is far less expensive both in time and money. Your city or town may have a local Center for Adult Education or Learning Annex where, in half a dozen Thursday evenings for $100 or $200, you can learn a great deal about using QuickBooks, setting up your own website or blog, planning for start-up costs, or filing a business tax return. A call to the local SCORE (Service Corps of Retired Executives) or Small Business Development Center may even help you to find a knowledgeable volunteer who could sit down with you every couple of weeks for your first few months to help you get started and demystify cash flow planning, licensing and permits, getting your sales and federal tax numbers, establishing banking, credit, and payment processing services, identifying and meeting your insurance, accounting, and legal needs, and organizing for record keeping and tax deductions.

In order to get the most out of such possibilities, I recommend that you comport yourself, in approaching them, as "The Person Who Can Learn from Others." If you come across as a full-of-yourself know-it-all, you better know it all, because no one is likely to offer you much help.

While I am about the process of offering bromides and platitudes here, let me further suggest that it is wise to set very conservative, manageable goals to begin with. It is exciting to set your goals high, but it can be colossally disappointing when harsh realities present themselves. If you set your goals a little bit lower, it can be very satisfying to meet them, and perhaps even to blow them away.

I have no doubt that, if enough people read this book, some readers will slam it because they somehow conclude that I am holding out the independent author-publisher model as a get-rich-quick scheme. Please! Stop! Slam me if you wish to slam me, but do not be confused: independent publishing is not a likely way to get rich quick.

In fact, it's time to disclose a dirty little secret here. Although I have been trumpeting the little cultural revolutions of indie film and indie music over the past few decades, neither of these movements nor an independent publishing movement are a road map to riches for artists of any stripe. What these movements have enabled is affordable production processes, new distribution paths, and a certain readiness on the part of a loosely defined potential audience, but these conditions do not, in and of themselves, guarantee commercial success. Nor should they.

Dealing with Negativity

How you deal either with negativity may depend on where it comes from, on what kind of writing you do, on your overall mindset and approach to your work, and on the thickness of your skin. There is a certain amount of negative sniping that comes with the territory when an author ventures onto the web. Snarky customer reviews or blog "comments" may reflect and reveal more about the commenter than about the content about which they are commenting. Whether they are motivated by jealousy, a bad day, buyer's remorse, general grumpiness, a misguided desire by the commenter to elevate his own stature at your expense, or some other agenda or pathology, the good news is that much of your desired audience is well equipped to see right through them. As long as they do not occur too frequently, you should ignore them.

However, if such comments begin to occur frequently or dominate your web presence, they can create problems. Let me use a personal example to illustrate the need to pay attention.

Soon after the Kindle was launched in mid-November 2007, I published an article for whom the target audience was the new and growing population of Kindle owners. Sales quickly took off, reflecting the fact that the piece was professionally presented, that it came up at the top of many Kindle searches, and that it received some positive word of mouth on Kindle-related blogs. By early February the piece was in the Kindle store bestseller list's top ten titles, and had sold over 2,000 "copies." However, contrary to any advice I would ever give to another author, I had paid no attention to generating positive customer comment, and I would soon pay for it.

In mid-February four very brief, negative, one-star reviews showed up in a matter of a few days. Their tone and structure suggested that the reviewers may well have been, at the very least, in contact with each other. I soon was able to sleuth out the fact that two of them were written by the same non-fan. The gist of his critique was basically that any technically proficient Kindle owner could figure out what the article presented with a little work, that the article was consequently not worth its $2.39 price, and that I had obviously figured out how to make a great deal of money from Kindle owners. Food for thought, certainly.

Since these reviews showed up in a very short period of time, the sniper-reviewer(s) succeeded in accomplishing what I assume was [their] goal. My 5-star rating fell to 3 stars, and my sales of the article in question quickly dropped off by about 40 percent. I decided that action was overdue.

Several people had commented positively about the article via email, so I began with them. I encouraged them to post reviews, and a couple did. I also decided to take a few steps to beef up the article's content. I was already confident in its quality, substance, and the fact that it was worth at least as much as a venti coffee o' the day. But why not make it even more valuable to my readers? I added several additional pages of good, dense content.

But I also realized that by not asking for positive reviews I had been flying naked, easy prey for snipers of any stripe. For good and obvious reasons, Amazon does not tell authors or publishers who buys their titles, so it is not like you can send each reader a thank-you note bundled with a review request. Instead, I added a "prefatory note to readers" to the content of the article, in which I offered to send any interested reader the content as a Word document, so they could view it on their screen while they experimented with its tips on their Kindles. All that they would need to do was send me an email with "Please send tips" in the subject line. I now receive a couple of dozen or so such requests each week. With each Word attachment that I send out, I include a note thanking them for their interest, along with a gentle postscript in which I encourage them, if they liked the article, to post a review.

Writing a review directly from your Kindle is not a simple or obvious thing to do unless you have very tiny thumbs, so I am asking readers to take an extra step and log into Amazon on their computers, so I do not expect a high-percentage yield. But each week now I receive a half-dozen or so new 5-star reviews, my customers' rating has recovered nicely, and my sales have recovered to the point where the article has been among the top three sellers in the Kindle store for the past couple of months. It's been good for sales, and even better for my peace of mind.

PART THREE:

UNLEASHING A 21ST-CENTURY
INDIE MOVEMENT
OF READERS AND WRITERS

Chapter III.1

Monkey Shakespeare and the Myth
Of Publishing Gatekeepers
As Guardians of Excellence

We've all heard the one about the million monkeys. Sit a million monkeys down at a million keyboards for a million hours (or maybe it's forever), and you're bound to get *Hamlet*, or the *King James Bible*, or at least "Kublai Khan." Websites devoted to the idea have come and gone, with some using random number generation programs to simulate the typing efforts or more monkeys than we ever need fear as real-life literary competition. So far, according to what I have been able to discover, such simulators have burned up billions of monkey-years and the little rascals' best showing is a match of 23 words from *Timon of Athens*. Fortunately, these experiments have saved the monkey population and the rest of us a ton of dull reading by covering the back end of the proposition with text recognition and comparison programs. (There is no evidence to support rumors that Simon & Schuster is planning to roll out a version of the text recognition program to streamline its "editorial" offices later this year.)

Aside from its possessing a certain trippy but transitory intellectual charm, the Monkey Shakespeare notion never impressed me much. Of course, as a writer, I could never buy it, and furthermore I never thought it especially relevant in illuminating any intellectual terrain that interested me.

Until recently.

We've paid dearly for our complacency as readers. The colossal mountain of dreck being foisted upon the reading public by the mainstream publishing industry is an assault on all of us who are forced to wade through it in order to find something interesting and engaging to read. All of the publishers' power in marketing, message, bookstore placement, and the sheer size of their mega-unit print runs is orchestrated to tell us that we simply must read the latest bestsellers, and to keep practically secret the availability and appeal of, say, any small, possibly even literary gem released by City Lights or Akashic Books or TriQuarterly Press.

If we could teach a million monkeys to read as a way of facilitating the Monkey Shakespeare experiment, we could probably never get them to sit still for the dreck that the mainstream publishing industry is serving up. They would surely rebel.

I don't mean to compare Paris Hilton, Bill O'Reilly, and Danielle Steel to a million typing monkeys. The monkeys don't have spell-check.

But there is nothing dark and conspiratorial about the fact that most of the literary gatekeepers such as book reviewers and booksellers are in no position to help us wade through all of the hundreds of thousands of titles that appear each year. More often, they are simply overwhelmed. They are also economically dependent upon that same highly concentrated publishing industry, and it only natural, when faced with the fact that roughly 300,000 new titles are coming into print each year, that they should be drawn toward the titles that are getting the lion's share of the publishers' marketing budget budgets and the biggest print runs. The literary gatekeeper who sees her role as guiding a literary culture rather than merely reflecting mass culture is becoming ever more rare.

Okay, so my lame effort to milk something meaningful from the "million monkeys" illustration has surpassed even my own eccentric sense of what is an acceptable level of goofiness in otherwise serious discourse. I apologize. Maybe I should have tried, instead, to draw something useful from the old Springsteen song, "57 Channels and Nothing On."

* * *

Most of us have long since made some settlement with the culture at large. We are free, we think, to enjoy what we enjoy. There is, after all, no end of browsing opportunities: we have libraries, bookstores, online bookselling websites, book clubs, competing online archives that may someday search every book ever written, and the considerable book departments of Wal-Mart, BJs, Target, Costco, Super Stop & Shop, Buck-a-book, and Building 19. We are the recipients or targets of buzz and marketing and book reviews or commentary in the newspapers, magazines, on television and the radio and podcasts, in the mail, and of course, online. There have never been so many books published each year, so many books in print, and so many books available through so many distribution channels.

If we wish to read books that are edgy, experimental, or in some way avant-garde, or books that appeal mostly to some specific niche audience, we might well celebrate the diversity of selections available. Poetry chapbooks? Political tomes? Philosophical treatises? Anthems to unleash movements? Fantasy novels with strong female protagonists? Quality varies, but most of these are published by, at least, the hundreds each year, and we also have choices as to whether we want them new or used, in printed books or downloadable e-books, text or audio, and so forth.

With such a range of choices available to us, then, why should we be snobs about the books that are published for others? If Ann Coulter wants to write a book expounding upon her infantile political views, and people want to read it, God forbid anyone should claim they are not well within their rights. If Jenna Jameson slaves away in her garret to bang out a volume of wit and wisdom accumulated during her career as the star of dozens of XXX-rated sex films, and it climbs athwart Ms. Coulter's book near the top of the *New York Times* bestseller lust, we may make a wry observation or two, but why should we conclude that our own interests have been negatively affected?

* * *

In the Fall of 2004, some of the book publishing industry's more recognizable mouthpieces worked themselves into a major lather over the short list of five finalist's for that year's National Book Award for Fiction. None of the five nominees were, to put it mildly, best sellers. The *New York Times* subjected the nominees to at least three separate "lump them all together" drive-by literary assassinations, in which *Times* staffers found various ways to damn all five books for a variety of closely related sins. The major publishing houses' spokespersons were especially shrill in their attacks both on the nominees as authors and on the five-judge National Book Award fiction nominating panel.

In a lengthy "Critic's Notebook" piece under the snarky headline "Book Award Becomes a Feast of Canapés," the *Times* bathed the five nominated fiction books in some distinctly double-edged coverage. All five book covers were shown in full-color graphics large enough to allow the titles to be read, and the jump-page runover text was decked with black and white head shots of the five authors, but what was most notable in these graphic displays was a short line of text under each title that purported to show each books sales-to-dates at the time of the article's publication. Sarah Shun-lien Bynum's *Madeleine is Sleeping* (Harcourt) had "sold" a reported 1,500 copies, Lily Tuck's *The News from Paraguay* (Harper Collins) 900, Kate Walbert's *Our Kind* (Scribners) 2,800, Christine Schutt's *Florida* (TriQuarterly) just 340, and Joan Silber's *Ideas of Heaven* (Norton) an even thousand. A tiny line of print further down sourced the sales data as coming from Nielsen BookScan and disclaimed "Figures do not reflect all retail sales; not included are sales to consumers through publishers' Web sites, by authors at non-bookstore signings, or library purchases."

The various reporters and columnists who weighed in in the pages of the *Times* and its *Sunday Times Book Review* section seemed demonstrably disappointed that the five nominees were not *Moby Dick, Ulysses, Middlemarch, Don Quixote,* and *Portnoy's Complaint.* There was precious little evidence that any of the contributing journalists had actually read the nominated books, but a lack of close textual analysis did not impede their sniping:

* "There's such a tyranny of white space in these already short books that a chapter running a few pages feels like *War and Peace.*"

* "When the fiction nominees were announced, there was much grumbling about their sameness -- all women, all living in New York City, all little-known names."

* "[A]ll five are built upon compressed observations that easily veer into precious writers' program language, too woozy and poetic for its own good."

* "short-story aesthetic...."

* "anemic sales...."

Nobody complained of language that was "too poetic for its own good" a year earlier when the crisp stylist Stephen King received the foundation's annual medal for his distinguished lifelong contribution to American letters. Sometimes, as I read these journalists' reports about this controversy, I suspected that the greatest single failing of the five nominated women writers was that none of them was Philip Roth: "Philip Roth shouldn't automatically be nominated just for being Philip Roth," observed the *Times*' Solomon-like Edward Wyatt wisely in the concluding paragraph of his piece, "but he shouldn't be punished for it either."

A couple of the nominated books were, alas, short story collections, and all of them were described by *Times* staffers as "small" works of fiction (like *The Old Man and the Sea*, one guesses, or *Dubliners* or *Their Eyes Were Watching God*). In a *New York Times Book* review essay that was teased with a cover headline "Fiction prizes that kill fiction," Laura Miller dismissed the five books by driving an interesting, if rather snobbish, wedge between readers and writers: "Readers, as a rule, care more about what an author writes; other writers are often more impressed with how. Beautiful sentences, formal experiments and infinitely delicate evocations of emotional states abound in these five books, but those woebegone souls in search of a good story will have to keep looking, elsewhere."

Whatever the lowest-common-denominator norm of "just the facts, ma'am" readers envisioned in this description, it was bracing to see it accepted, even celebrated, in the pages of the *Times Book Review*.

Miller was not alone in making a larger polemical point about the award nominees. "Using the National Book Awards to bring attention to fine but overlooked novels is a noble plan, perhaps, but one undercut by the fact that it doesn't really work," she wrote with biting assertiveness. "The list tends to get received not as a recommendation but as a rebuke: these are the great books you *should* have been reading and the press *should* have been covering when you were wasting your time and column inches on safe big-name talents and inferior crowd-pleasers, you vulgarians."

Time Warner Book Group chairman Larry Kirschbaum was quoted in at least two *Times* articles saying that the publishing industry is "supporting our demise" by continuing to finance awards that do not honor the big publishers' marketing decisions and investments. One can't help but wonder, of course, whether these apologists for the mega-publishers, in singing such well-synchronized tunes from a common hymnal (or talking points?) weren't protesting too much. If "it doesn't really work," how can it be "supporting our demise"? Another critic said that all five books were written in "precious writing program language" -- not the kind of prose one finds in a good Grisham or Clancy, one guesses -- and one chapter of nominee Sarah Shun-lien Bynum's *Madeleine is Sleeping* is singled out for ridicule ("a tyranny of white space"!) because it is only five words long.

Maybe this is just me, but as I read the *Times*' various pieces over the course of several weeks that Fall, with their gratuitously repetitive references to the writers' shared gender, I began to suspect I was being invited to dismiss the fiction nominees as not only "small" and "literary," but as "small and literary in a female way," a way that Norman Mailer might be helpful in deconstructing were he still with us. Some other recent award winners in this category also live in New York and compose rather literary sentences, but Jonathan Franzen is a man, and on top of that he is a man who can go on for over 500 pages, as none of these women apparently can. And as for the previous year's recipient of the National Book Award's version of the Oscar for lifetime achievement, at least nobody is likely to complain of a "tyranny of white space" in Mr. King's books.

While reasonable people may disagree about the quality or appeal of individual works of art, the key industry spokespersons who were quoted in these Times articles were obviously aghast that the fiction nominating committee was conspiring in the destruction of the publishing industry:

* "We are completely closing ourselves off from the culture at large," said Kirschbaum.

* "We are not helping the book business this way, and we're not exactly flourishing already," said frequent Don Imus radio guest Esther Newberg, then a literary agent at International Creative Management.

* "I can't imagine what the conversation was that produced these results," said former Random House editorial director Jason Epstein, who seemed chagrined primarily that Roth's *The Plot Against America* had escaped notice despite its blockbuster promotional budget and print run.

What the industry was really pandering for, quite shamelessly, was that the literary culture should line up behind the mass culture as reflected in the marketing decisions of the big publishers, validate their choices by stamping another of these big books with its prize imprimatur whenever possible, and help prop up it flagging sales rather than call attention to a handful of writers who are never going to become brand-name bestsellers anyway. There is an impressive Orwellian sophistication in any marketing scheme that is able to convince otherwise intelligent journalists that it is supporting creativity and quality in the face of so much evidence that it is, in fact, feeding a culture that is utterly commercial and undiscriminating.

To their credit, the nominated writers -- did I mention that they are all women? -- showed a little feistiness of their own. Finalist Christine Schutt (*Florida*), asked to comment on critic John Leonard's suggestion that a prize winner should be someone who has "put in time" and "paid his dues," stood up nicely: "I am 56. I have taught literature at a girls' school in Manhattan, Nightingale-Bamford, for more than 20 years. My first collection was titled *Nightwork* because I wrote it at night while I was divorced and raising two sons. How else can I pay my dues?"

In her Sunday book review essay, Miller did not back up her rather counter-intuitive claim, that the National Book Award serve as a rebuke rather than a recommendation and do not bring attention to otherwise overlooked novels, with any market analysis or data points of any kind. Her claims were easier to sustain, coming as they did in the weeks before the final prize winner was announced, than they would have been later when all five nominees, and especially winner Lily Tuck's *Paraguay*, were selling nicely for debut or early literary fiction after their short-list sales bump.

It is not a matter of one side in this controversy being right and the other being wrong, despite my obvious bias, because there is, one hopes, no unassailable and non-subjective means for anyone asserting that one novel or book of short stories is better than another. We all have our tastes, or lack thereof, and over time we tend to identify others whose tastes we come to trust or find interesting or provocative, and we attend to what they have to say. But whatever their tastes, the rationales that underpin the publishers' minor tantrum in this controversy ought to diffuse rather than intensify any cultural hegemony they have hitherto earned as tastemakers. And by adhering so closely to the lesser angels of their economic self-interests, they may have likely have caused more than a few readers and writers to ponder for ourselves where our own interests lie, and whether book manufacturers speak better for those interests than we might speak ourselves.

Ultimately, the central polemical point of this modest little book is that writers and readers have a powerful cultural and economic interest in standing up together, contra the literary-industrial complex, to steer the literary culture as much as we can, rather than merely to reflect, as the major publishers do, the mass culture. In that context, if the five members of the National Book Award fiction nominating committee for 2004 -- Rick Moody, Linda Hogan, Randall Kenan, Stewart O'Nan, and Susan Straight -- were carrying out a subversive agenda in making their short-list nominations, more power to them!

It also seemed telling that, in the opening sentence of the same piece, Wyatt chose to dismiss one of the books for its weak sales: "Perhaps the 150 or so people who have bought Christine Schutt's first novel, *Florida*, will agree that it may be the year's best book," sniffed Wyatt, somehow knocking down by more than half the 340 copies noted in the *Times* graphic. (Schutt, in an interview a couple of weeks later with the *Times Sunday* magazine's Deborah Solomon, was placed in the not very appealing position of having to protest that "*Florida* has actually sold at least 1,099 copies."

So what is really going on here?

First, give credit where it is due. Harcourt, Scribners, Norton, and Harper Collins deserve kudos, along with Northwestern University Press' TriQuarterly Books imprint, for publishing five distinguished books of fiction.

But the fact that these books were initially put out there without even an ounce of promotional muscle or marketing strategy condemned them to a lottery where it was virtually guaranteed that they would lose money as publishing projects. What were the publishers thinking? That Oprah Winfrey or Deirdre Imus would pick them up and read them? That they would make the National Book Award short list?

Unfortunately, with the exception of books by celebrity or brand-name authors, the major publishers no longer seem to know how to promote their own best books unless they happen to receive one of those dream imprimaturs, and the competition for them is fierce. All but the most predictable bestsellers tend to get lost in the shuffle, in an industry that is often disorganized, non-entrepreneurial, and thinly staffed by interns and recent college graduates who possess little knowledge or credibility when it comes to guerilla (or any other form of) marketing. The publishers do seem to understand that it would be best if some notion of literary quality could remain associated with their brand identity, but the operational result of this fuzzy awareness is that they look to the National Book Award for Fiction to provide them with artistic cover while they continue to pursue purely commercial objectives.

Frequently it falls to authors to take most of the responsibility for marketing their own books, but they often begin with three strikes against them:

* They don't know much of anything about marketing;

* They are frequently lulled into thinking that their publishers will handle all that; and

* They are squeamish about self-promotion because of a literary as well as a more general culture that stigmatizes anyone who actually tries to sell books.

"Publication is not the proper business of poets," is how Miss Dickinson, the Belle of Amherst, put it.

Easy for her to say!

That approach is not working, and it badly needs an overhaul.

Authors, readers, and publishers all have a common interest in wiping out these cultural stigmata so that we all recognize authors as having the same right and need to promote their own work and engage their own audiences that we happily accord, for instance, to independent musicians and filmmakers.

Meanwhile, it does no good to blame the big publishing houses for betting so much of their budgets on "guaranteed bestsellers." They cannot help themselves, and in the long run they are the losers in their own bargain. Every time some global conglomerate lays out several hundred million Euros to overpay for a publishing house, they commit themselves to stratospheric future profit benchmarks in order to justify the amortized purchase price, and they add layers of administrative cost that become part of every book's required overhead contribution without adding much of anything to a book's commercial or marketing muscle. At the time of acquisition the acquiring company sends out its top corporate ambassadors to assure the publishing house employees that the parent company will maintain its commitment to its publishing mission, while trying not to get into too much detail about any non-commercial goals. But eventually the numbers will rule, and it will become very difficult at the conglomerate's highest levels to justify the publication of new authors or literary work. Even if a single editor decides that a literary work has real merit, she must succeed in a difficult campaign of persuasion, and that manuscript can be blown out of the water by another decision-maker's lack of passion for the project.

A few throwback editors endure here and there, but they find themselves surrounded increasingly by colleagues who have been forced to see the light: hit the numbers or hit the bricks. And the formula for hitting the numbers is all too clear in an industry with little tolerance or financial margin for small-scale efforts: find a guaranteed brand-name bestseller, lock in a 500,000-copy print run to flood the market, sell off the film, mass market paperback, and foreign rights, back it all up with a six-figure marketing budget, and don't worry about it until next year if the reviews turn out bad, the reading public gets fed up with cookie-cutter schlock, and you have to remainder half the hardcovers and destroy half the paperbacks. By then, you can always scour the *Publishers Weekly* ads for an opening at another house.

Problem is, even though the basic building blocks of this formula can be distilled from some of the publisher's greatest success stories, there is little about this approach that is well thought out as a long-term strategy. As the internet expands the transparency of all markets and the power of grassroots buzz and word of mouth, both positive and negative, any publishing strategy that places a higher value on hype than on quality, and that repeatedly promises more than it delivers, is bound to atrophy its own reader base. Paris Hilton's remarkable belly button, and the stunning expanse between it and the top of her occasional bottomwear, may sell a few books, but she is no Madonna.

It is symptomatic of much deeper cultural ailments, which will not be quickly cured, that so many Americans are so fascinated with news niblets, factoids, and writings by or about O.J. Simpson, Bill O'Reilly, and Michael Jackson. There should not be any doubt that these trends will continue and that profit-hungry mega-publishers as well as the rest of the mass media will continue to engorge us, and in turn, themselves, with this fare. But there is something both pathetic and alarming when this same publishing industry tries to turn the tables and demand a corporate welfare tribute from the literary culture, as happened or was at least suggested (with professional courtesy shilling services from the *New York Times*) during the 2004 National Book Award controversy.

Chapter III.2

THE FEEDBACK IS THE FILTER: WHO WILL DISTINGUISH QUALITY IN AN INDIE PUBLISHING FUTURE?

Now that we have seen how technological advances such as the Kindle, CreateSpace, and [*insert Next Big Thing here*] make it possible for authors and independent publishers to bring their work to readers (and, yes, "to market") without any significant financial investment (except for the obvious fact that time is money), it is important to bring the focus back to where we started in this book: to issues of quality and distinction.

Have you ever wondered how, before the rise of the publishing industry and the *New York Times Book Review*, cultures managed to confer distinction on quality literary work? Who told the Beowulf poet, if not to keep "writing," exactly, then at least to keep composing? Who told an earlier bard: "Keep up the fine work, Homer! You'll need a good editor, but I think I hear a single!"

The processes by which cultures filter and distinguish between quality artistic work and lesser efforts are constantly subject to their own reversals, second-guessing, and border wars. At times these processes are not so different either from a game of "king of the mountain" among ten-year-olds, or from the process by which religious sects confer the status of "messiah" or "madman" on someone who walks the earth making unexpected pronouncements.

One's acceptance (or not) of a jury's judgments will always be intrinsically tethered to, and will sometimes inform, one's considerations about that jury's composition. Controversies over who gets to serve as a culture's jury become especially fierce when the culture is undergoing major structural changes as a result of changes in audience, artistic process, and the means of production and dissemination employed by the culture's various media.

But this relationship between the "what's worth reading?" question and the question of "who thinks so?" is not a simple one. Even if we could agree on what constitutes excellent writing (which we can't), there would be myriad other considerations of lesser or greater importance to individual readers. Beyond the domain of the relatively small number of books that become bestsellers, there are hundreds of thousands of books and authors with smaller but still significant followings based on genre, topic, style, personal loyalties, their linkages with other books and reading communities, and, of course, their quality as received and registered by individual readers. In a "long-tail" literary world where there is a seemingly limitless choice of individual titles, what we must do to find the books that we want to read is changed dramatically and depends on the ways in which we, and the cultural marketplaces that we frequent, are organized into tribes and sub-tribes of readers and writers. But before we explore that Googlezon present and future, a look at where we have been may help us to be clear about what there is to lose and to gain in the transformations that are shaking the 21st-century publishing world.

In the grand early- and mid-20th century world of American publishing, the Olympian judgments of venerable publishing houses such as Scribners and Alfred Knopf were accepted, by and large, by writers, readers, and other gatekeepers and tastemakers of the book trade such as critics and booksellers. Most authors trusted editors and agents to give fair consideration to their submissions and to make selections that corresponded in some discernible way to their relative quality, even if anti-artistic censorship led occasionally to the temporary suppression of distinguished efforts such as *Ulysses, Lolita, Lady Chatterley's Lover,* or *Howl*. The fact that the publishing industry was overwhelmingly a white man's world was but a sad mirror of similar barriers that flawed the society at large. And although it frequently did not deliver on its promises, "the life of the writer" often seemed to promise a way out of many ghettoes of race, gender, class, and psychopathology.

Authors such as Hemingway and Faulkner enjoyed special status as literary celebrities, with face time on the cover of *Time* and work excerpted or serialized in widely read magazines such as The *Saturday Evening Post* or *Collier's*. This mass culture validated, reflected, and extended the literary culture, and several such authors enjoyed the kind of popular status that later became the terrain of rock stars, respected at times for literary achievement but just as often for their legends as rugged (or not) individualists who rose by their own remarkable efforts to live lives that inspired a kind of *Lifestyles of the Literary Rich and Famous* envy or emulation.

The fact that the mass culture was able to provide fair representation of the literary culture is testimony to the poverty of each in their common homogeneity. Still and all, 20th century literature often broadened and illuminated the human experience, helped us to fathom if not always to embrace the ghastly and lovely and banal range of human behavior, and seemed often to anticipate or give form to nearly every preoccupation of the species. The incubation and development of writers has never been precisely a democratic process, even with respect to opportunity, but these paths appeared accessible to so many that "to become a writer" became at once a lifestyle dream, a therapeutic cure (or enabler), and one of the world's most glorious and widely held career objectives. The overall selection processes seemed fair or seamless or logically Darwinian enough that both authors and audience tended to trust and accept the roles of editors, agents, and other gatekeepers. Such trust was based on several key assumptions:

· manuscripts submitted to agents and editors would usually get a reading, and a fair reading to boot;

· agents would make a serious effort to sell any work they arranged to represent;

· there would be a rough and uneven yet still plausible correspondence between those works accepted for publication and those deemed to have either literary quality or commercial viability or both, underpinned by a widely shared if sentimental trust that the publishing world was well-populated with individuals genuinely committed to pushing the equation whenever possible in the direction of literary quality; and

· once a book was accepted for publication, its publisher would make a serious effort to market it so that it would stand a fair chance of getting inclusion and notice in the thousands of independent bookstores that were as ubiquitous then as hardware stores and in the literary periodicals that reviewed a much larger selection of literary work than they consider nowadays.

None of the foregoing assumptions has survived recent dramatic changes in the publishing industry. Only a tiny percentage of outsiders' manuscript submissions sent to agents and editors gets even a cursory reading now. Pragmatic agents often see it as a quixotic enterprise even to submit literary fiction, narrative nonfiction, or other good work to the major publishing houses unless something about them nearly guarantees bestseller status. These houses are so driven by the need for scalable revenues and high turnover bestsellers that literary quality or enduring cultural value usually takes a distant back seat to considerations about whether an author has a marketable brand-name (think Paris Hilton, Danielle Steel, Jenna Jameson, or Tom Clancy) or a powerful cross-media sales platform (think Bill O'Reilly, Ann Coulter, Dr. Phil, or Sean Hannity).

These failures of the mainstream publishing industry and its gatekeepers to meet the cultural and economic needs of readers and writers might lead in any event to challenges to the traditional roles of judge and jury in our literary culture. But part of the publishing companies' power also accrues from a mighty self-censoring tendency among many writers, a walking-on-eggshells phenomenon that Jonathan Franzen, in his essay collection *How to Be Alone*, has aptly described as "the idea ...

that cultural complaint is pathetic and self-serving in writers who don't sell, ungracious in writers who do."

Underlying these issues of fairness and sensibility is a more fundamental sea change that guarantees the continuing transformation of the publishing industry. Whatever its grandeur, much of American culture in the middle decades of the 20th century was built on assumptions of stunning homogeneity. In music, literature, film, television, and politics the only significant differences recognized by the mass culture were generational, and any cultural expressions on the "other" side of the culture's primary racial divides were, to white audiences, for all intents and purposes "underground."

In contrast, we now swim in a sea of limitless cultural choices. Although the explosions of the internet and digital technologies are the primary enabling forces for the existence of this long-tail world, its mere existence is not its most significant distinction. More importantly, a remarkable confluence of forces has created an active appetite for such a wide array of choices. These forces include the early indie movements in music and film, the political ferment of the sixties, changes in educational approach and, most importantly, the growth of the internet as a social and cultural networking infrastructure.

While the mainstream mega-publishers seem bound by economics and their own retrograde pre-occupation with bestsellers to fall short of satisfying the growing appetite for choice, independent publishers and entrepreneurial indie authors are well-situated to respond. Small, fast-moving publishers and authors can respond to niche needs and tribal tastes not only in fiction, poetry, and literary nonfiction but also in a wide array of other nonfiction categories.

At the most recent turn of the century, important advances in technology and the marketplace were empowering independent-minded writers and pushing the publishing world toward, if not a precipice, a significant tipping point:

· First, digitized print technologies made quality short-run book manufacturing so inexpensive that an independent publisher could surpass the production break-even point with a printing of 2,000 to 3,000 copies of a paperback original and a sell-through of as few as a third of the print run; and

· second, such publishers gained easy, inexpensive access to a gathering critical mass of sales and distribution channels including their own websites, the Amazon Advantage program, the Internet's thousands of independent third-party booksellers, and a critical mass of independent bookstores and libraries. Wholesalers such as Baker & Taylor and Quality Books began to work proactively with small publishers and some short-run book manufacturers began to offer their small-publisher customers reliable bundles of ancillary services such as warehousing, fulfillment, distribution, order processing, regular inventory and sales reporting, and collections.

More recent developments have only intensified the velocity of change: with the advent of the Amazon Kindle and Amazon's CreateSpace publishing platform in 2007, authors and publishers can bring literature "to market" at little or no cost, and even more importantly, with immediate connectivity to potent established markets and distribution channels that lead to millions of readers.

Each of these developments is likely to subvert traditional gatekeeping roles in the publishing industry. Will they also subvert the literary culture itself by committing it to a relentless downward spiral in quality, cheapening and "democratizing" what is available in book or any other form to the point where quality written work goes begging because it is lost in a swamp of mediocrity? Although I personally welcome, and include myself in the ranks of, an independent publishing movement, I do not diminish the importance or reasonableness of this concern about quality. I must admit to being less sanguine on this issue than former Random House editor Jason Epstein, one of the most respected elders of the American publishing industry, who wrote in his thoughtful 2001 volume, *Book Business: Publishing Past Present Future*, that "these new technologies will test the human capacity to distinguish value from a wilderness of choice, but humanity has always faced this dilemma and solved it well enough over time.... The filter that distinguishes value is a function of human nature, not of particular technologies."

But we are fortunate to have particular technologies to give human nature an assist. The internet offers a viral post-advertising expansion of communication channels and platforms by which readers may communicate not only with each other but also inter-actively with writers, publishers, booksellers, and librarians about the content and quality of books and other media. Within these protean networks all advertising is forbidden but almost any medium can carry, in its DNA, an acceptable alternative to marketing.

There is much for an indie publishing movement to emulate in the processes by which the "do-it-yourself" spirit in music and film during the last two or three decades has broken through to build a kind of positive if generic "brand" distinction for "indie" maverick movements in their own right, as compared with the self-publisher's "vanity press" stigma that must be overcome by independent book publishers. It is no accident that one of the more articulate voices promoting an indie book publishing movement, editor-in-chief Johnny Temple of Akashic Books, would write in a recent *Poets & Writers* article that "I entered the book business through the portal of underground rock music.

"The idea," wrote Temple in describing the musicians' indie movement, "was that hardworking bands, upstart record labels (often launched by musicians) and dedicated fans could forge a vital, idealistic alternative to the mainstream music business." The importance of those "dedicated fans" should not be underestimated; writers, publishers, booksellers, librarians, and mindful readers should seek out every available opportunity to cultivate vehicles for reader communication, reader-writer contact, and reader self-identification with an indie movement of writers and publishers. Both in the physical world of reading groups, bookstore readings, library discussion groups, and Oprah segments and in the web world of book blogs, meet-ups, online social networking sites and Amazon customer reviews, the potential for such interaction is exploding far more dramatically than the population base of physical or digital book readers is atrophying. Writers' groups, which tend as it is to function simultaneously as readers' groups, would do well to seek out any chance to broaden their base and replicate or extend themselves as reader-writer affinity groups. One can easily imagine the Kindle itself, with its huge (and mostly still untapped) potential for file-sharing, annotation, and networking, as a primary hub for such communities if future price breaks and next-generation input enhancements allow.

Even in a cultural environment such as the blogosphere – a seeming narcissist's paradise where the ego-gratification of traffic and comment is instant and almost every reader is also a writer – literary culture is braced by forces that are, in one sense, as old-fashioned as book discussion groups or the knowledgeable independent bookseller whose recommendations join her wide reading experience with her understanding of her customers' reading interests and tastes. Yet as old-school as they may be in basic form, the internet recapitulators of these natural outcroppings of human nature can be almost unimaginably more powerful because they are also viral, instantaneous, and global.

Readers and book browsers in every age have wanted to know, in evaluating whether to take a chance (either with their time or their money, or both) on a book, how many others are reading it, who they are, and what they think of it. This information serves not only to send signals about quality; it also feeds a deep and powerful tribal urge for many readers. They want to read books (or see movies or hear music) that will spark and perhaps elevate their social and intellectual interactions with others, and when they read good books they want to seek out people with whom they can discuss the books, their ideas, their characters, and so forth. Disclosing one's reading, musical, and film tastes has become such an automatic self-branding ritual that, in addition to helping to bring you new recommendations for a book to read on Sunday morning, the act may also help you to find a date on Saturday night.

Just as buzz breeds buzz, the process by which sales success breeds sales success is not limited to those permutations that involve readers (or all the book trade's gatekeepers) noting a title on the *New York Times* bestseller list and then making room for it in their own plans. On the internet, whether in book blogs, among the apparently democratic and accessible book review and rating templates to be found on Amazon.com or its emulators, or in countless other venues yet to be imagined, the information that a title is selling well is instantly available, easy to use, and all the more likely, because of its own seemingly transparent and unmediated character, to serve as a quality filter or signaling system for readers and for all the other aforementioned gatekeepers of the book trade. The natural consequence of these processes in our hit-obsessed culture will be to ensure that we will always have bestsellers, perhaps even long after we have book publishers in the traditional sense, even if over time the sales requirements for attaining such status are somewhat moderated.

For all of its fertility as a vineyard for individual creativity and differentiated voices, the web is also an elegantly complex yet exquisitely simple binary world where, as with the inner meta-biology of the human brain, content and process may eventually be equivalent. Every word that is typed, read, linked, or clicked becomes traffic and velocity, and every hit is its own unmediated form of comment, and therefore of content. Every time we tag, visit, rate, buy, link, bookmark, download, sample or otherwise engage content, let alone when we write a comment or customer review or include it in our blog or blogroll, we are buzzing: asserting that certain content appeals to us or appalls us or bores us and may have a similar effect on others in the various tribes or networks to which we belong. We often choose these groups on the basis of the shared appeal of certain content; indeed they often spring up on an ad hoc basis around certain authors or books, certain musicians or films, etc. Importantly, given the leisure-time deficits with which many of us live, the bar of participation can be set as high or as low as we like.

These processes are as important for audience as they are for artists. It is obviously my intention here to be an advocate for the kind of cultural citizenship or activism that helps to define and organize the tribes and literary affinity groups of which we have been speaking, and to sort and distinguish the work of authors and other creators. I will always encourage people to exercise their rights as audience members in these ways and to recognize that the infrastructures of Amazon, Google, YouTube, iTunes, MySpace and countless other websites are so effective and seamless that – in ways that are so automatic that they may deserve the phrase "whether we like it or not" – we are all buzz agents.

What was that I called you? Well, pardon my presumption. You may not have a marketing bone in your body, but you are a rare individual if you haven't weighed in with others on a few of the following topics: books, politics, music, film, cars, television, technology, destinations, sneakers, swimming holes, food, restaurants, bars, businesses, business models, magazines, babysitters, schools, fashion, driving directions, or plumbers. We learn early on how to influence others and how to find value for ourselves in the influence of others, with varying degrees of mindfulness and vigilance about the process depending on the forum in which it is occurring, the self-presentation of others, and our individual natures. Increasingly, as our culture gets meaner and more cynical, we are distrustful of influences that appear to be directly commercial, only to find that the marketing wizards are spending billions on buzz that is indirectly commercial. We may think that it is at the point when we have to stop and apply a bullshit detector to all this buzz that we have left Eden, but the truth is that we have not been to Eden for a while.

Being a lover of books and reading, a bibliophile, early in the 21st Century, often means being a pro-active and curious inquisitor, scouting out writers that appeal to you among the offerings of trusted authors, small presses and literary magazines, the remaining independent bookstores, reading groups, Amazon reviews, and book blogs. It often means making early commitments to the careers of authors you love and tracking every printed or digitized word they produce. It may even mean giving up a smidgen of your intellectual privacy, whether to your local bookseller or librarian or to the algorithm aces at Amazon.com, in order to allow them to use their gifts at what the marketing mavens call "collaborative filtering" to help you, who loved the book of Richard Ford stories you read on the beach last summer, to find a Ray Carver selection to read this summer.

I have no doubt, as one who has satisfied his own reading appetites through various combinations of these and other means for the past few decades, that a large part of what motivates us as book scouts and buzz agents is the joy of discovery and then the gratification and validation of sharing what we discover with those with whom we sense some common ground: "Eureka! I've been reading the most wonderful book! I'll pass it on to you as soon as I've finished." However much we may experience the reading itself as either solitary or, in connection with the author, dyadic, it can also become, with our bibliophile soul mates, satisfyingly social. And in our internet age, we can carry out these interactions either locally or globally.

As with most other scouting enterprises, scouting for good books to read – and especially for books that suit our very individual reading needs -- is often a two-way street. The more we "speak," the more we will "hear." The more we listen, the more we will know about who we want to speak to, what to say to them, and what to ask them about. Along the way, we even learn a fair amount about how to conduct the conversation. One of the remarkable things about cultural marketplaces such as Amazon is the way in which they seem to train their visitors to become better and better at using the wealth of material that exists there to get their needs met.

Of course, to raise concerns about quality as if they only applied to the new forces in publishing is to beg the question regarding the performance of the traditional publishing institutions as defenders of literary quality. I am far from being the first writer to experience the relationships between authors (or, for that matter, readers) and the mainstream publishing industry as adversarial. I suspect that most of us, either chronically or episodically, are inclined to view almost anyone who tries to regulate our creative and cultural lives with some mixture of annoyance and contempt. If the issues that annoy us seem increasingly to be systemic rather than personal, then it is entirely appropriate for us to develop a sense of mission about the need to make things right. The mainstream publishing industry and its more Olympian apologists may prefer to cast such struggles as occurring between the guardians of publishing excellence and the rabble of artistic democracy, with the subtext that those in control, as much as they might like to suffer a thousand new flowers to bloom each publishing season, are, at the end of the day, the last remaining protectors of literary quality.

But all one must do is look around, in any chain bookstore or on the latest bestseller list, to conclude that, while the mainstream publishing industry may in some places have the elitist trappings of snobbish self-importance, it is not meritocratic in any way that is connected to literary quality. We note, without taking any pleasure in it, the fact that the quality filtering process that helped to make a bestseller of such a magnus opus as Jenna Jameson's ***How to Make Love Like a Porn Star*** or the latest scribblings of Paris Hilton or Rush Limbaugh is something less than meritocratic to begin with.

Once one determines that the big publishers could care less about quality at the expense of blockbuster bestsellers, it follows naturally that any renegade movement to allow independent creative people to make more of the decisions about what to publish and how to get that product into the hands of interested and discerning readers could be, and should be, less about artistic democracy than about artistic meritocracy and literary freedom. As growing numbers of writers accept the gifts and challenges of new technologies and our ubiquitous American entrepreneurial spirit and embark upon non-traditional publishing ventures to get their work before the reading public, we would be wise not to leave these issues of quality filtering, of "the cream rising to the top," either to the happenstances of human nature or to the vagaries of an untended marketplace. Along the way, some of us will be able to bring the universe of choices into smaller scale by connecting, if you will excuse my overburdening of that "cream to the top" metaphor, with consumers who prefer soy milk, goat's milk, buttermilk, and so forth.

For the self-interested author who believes that she has just self-published the next Great American Novel, the admonition in the previous paragraph may seem to be just another way of saying, "Don't just sit back and wait for the orders to start rolling in." But I mean to make a broader point: readers and writers, and especially those of us who locate ourselves vocationally anywhere in the literary culture, stand to benefit both directly and in a more general cultural sense by doing all we can to nurture those networks and informal associations that in one way or another honor, advance, and extend the market viability of literary work of distinction, of writing that is thoughtful, interesting, edgy, experimental, or, in the best sense of the word, ambitious. Perhaps this has always been true, but the stakes are higher now because the publishing industry at large is failing so miserably at these tasks and because, to be blunt, of the sheer volume of choices when something in the ballpark of 300,000 new titles is being printed each year.

There is already quite enough angst and hand-wringing about this flooding of the marketplace; I don't mean to suggest that any of us should posture or anoint ourselves as some sort of high-culture quality police. We can celebrate the candles without cursing the darkness, and I am much more troubled personally by the market flooding that is the result of the vast overprintings of individual titles, to the detriment both of the planet and of that quaint old phenomenon known as the mid-list title.

From here onward, there will be many good works, some in book form and some in shorter form that, because of the opportunities provided through the Kindle, the CreateSpace print-on-demand feature, and other yet-to-be-realized technologies, will be available "forever" and, absent any marketing, will sell usually in trickles of one or two each month, several each quarter. We can embrace this good fortune and, at the same time, be pleased that, much further out along the farthest reaches of the long tail, there will be works of the least significance and distinction, supported by the weakest of networks or no networks at all, that will exist only as onesies, twosies, or seldom-transmitted digital files. In the utter absence of buzz, quality, or usefulness, there will be only the sound of trees not having to fall in the forest because there is nobody there.

The moment may even come, as the role of the large commercially drive publishers declines, when one of those unreadable and unsellable titles will indeed be one that in another era might have been printed, remaindered, and ultimately destroyed by the hundreds of thousands. Of course we will never know when that elegantly silent moment occurs, but even without our being able to circle a date, I suggest that we should be able to celebrate its advent.

Chapter III.3

Rebel Distribution and Amazon's Marketplace of the Mind: You Need a Publisher Like a Fish Needs a Bicycle

Let's begin this chapter by reviewing the key functions or needs for which authors ***used to*** rely on publishers:

- Capital investment

- Printing

- Warehousing

- Fulfillment

- Access to distribution channels

- Marketing and promotion

- Payment of advances and royalties

- A publishing house "imprimatur" to confer distinction

The key words here, as you have already guessed, are "used to." As I am writing this, in 2008, authors simply have no need for publishers for any part of the first 6 functions listed above.

It is now no exaggeration to say that, with Amazon's CreateSpace and Kindle platforms, it is a snap to bring a book seamlessly, even elegantly, into the world's most powerful book distribution system, with the world's largest readership base, for nothing. No cost. No money.

When I say, "for nothing," it is natural to expect that there is another shoe waiting to drop. Surely, with respect to the CreateSpace print-on-demand process, you will have to set an exorbitant price for your book, and author royalties will be slight. Everybody knows that the economics of print-on-demand don't work, right?

No.

The fact is that the CreateSpace cost structure allows you to set reasonable paperback prices, like the price for the print-on-paper edition of this book, that are in line with the trade paperback prices of mainstream publishers. Then, on each individual book that you sell, CreateSpace costs are low enough that you will be able to make a profit margin far higher than what you would experience with any other print-on-demand vendor. CreateSpace economics are likely to force print-on-demand outfits such as iUniverse, xLibris, and AuthorHouse either to change their business models dramatically or to face a future as vanity publishers. Indeed, the CreateSpace pricing and costing structure would allow authors or publishers to experience profit margins just as high with CreateSpace as they would receive with short-run print runs in the 3,000-to-5,000 unit range. All, of course, without advancing a dime for printing, warehousing, fulfillment, or set-up fees. (For authors who require a little greater support and are willing or able to pay setup fees for it, the best choice is probably BookSurge, although Amazon would do better if it could avoid the appearance of bullying authors into using it. For authors or publishers who are looking for a high-quality, low-cost approach to short-run digital printing, warehousing, and fulfillment, I recommend contact with Tom Campbell at King Printing Company at www.adibooks.com).

One of the more stunning recent developments involving CreateSpace – which provides the same basic and economical template of print-on-demand services for music, other audio products, and film that it provides for book publishing – was the announcement in May 2008 that Amazon, Sony BMG and EMI Music would bring back hundreds of highly coveted out-of-print music albums on CD through CreateSpace "Disc on Demand" and offer the titles on Amazon.com.

So, let's drill down on this for just a moment. CreateSpace is now the choice of major record labels as the most economical way to produce and distribute backlist or out-of-print music. If, as I believe is true, the basic economics of CreateSpace CD production are about the same as CreateSpace book production, and if one of the challenges facing the best book publishers involves how to keep good mid-list and back-list titles in print at prices that will inspire some sales and allow some profit, it is clear where this leads. CreateSpace will soon be the print-and-distribution channel of choice for a growing number of quality publishers. For smaller literary publishers as well as for major publishing houses that still own extensive backlist rights, CreateSpace could even be a short-term but long-tail solution to waning profitability while publishers struggle to move beyond their clearly outmoded business models and adapt to 21st-century realities.

But for you and me or our favorite indie authors or thousands of other emerging writers, it is nice to know that we can compete with these publishers on a leveled playing field. If the economics of Kindle and Create Space work for these publishers, they will work for us, but we certainly have no need for the publishers to mediate our relationships with Kindle and CreateSpace, with Amazon, or with the growing millions of readers who visit Amazon's various websites each week.

The only questions that remain, of course, are whether it is worth a writer's efforts to secure the imprimatur of one of these publishing firms to distinguish his work. We will address these more qualitative issues in future chapters.

*   *   *

We have probably done justice to the Amazon Kindle already in previous chapters. The summary transitional points that I should make here are (1) that the Kindle will be very big, passing the 1-million mark for "Kindles in circulation" (and in the hands of proven, serious readers) by the second quarter of 2009, the 2-million mark by year-end 2009, and the 5-million mark in 2010 or 2011, and (2) even so, the Kindling population will represent just a tiny fraction of the reading public during the new years.

As the father of the self-publishing movement, Dan Poynter, has wisely pointed out, any author who is going to do the work to publish one or more books would be foolish not to extend that act to make the content in available in every medium to which it is naturally portable. The great news for every Kindle author and publisher is that once you have published your content for the Kindle, the additional steps required to extend your content to the printed page are simple and straightforward, with easy and helpful connectivity between the several distribution channels through which you will want to market your content in its various forms.

Once you've published a book in electronic form for the Kindle, you should seriously consider making it available in a print-on-paper edition. Rapid-fire changes in technology have brought us in the past decade from short-run digital press printing (where a competent author could do very well with two or three thousand copies for an initial capital outlay of about $5,000), to early, relatively inefficient print-on-demand technologies (that forced authors to set prices too high and pay expensive set-up costs), to an extremely smooth, inexpensive, and well-connected new print-on-demand program called CreateSpace that is now owned – and why should this surprise us? – by Amazon. Follow the same steps that are outlined in Chapter II.2 and they will serve you well in preparing for publishing on the CreateSpace platform, with the help of CreateSpace support pages and staff. In general, the CreateSpace functionality makes so much economic sense that we shouldn't be surprised if we find mainstream as well as indie publishers beginning to use it in the near future, just as major record labels are beginning to make significant deals with Amazon to re-issue out-of-print music through the CreateSpace music features.

The development of these new publishing technologies, combined with the rise of relatively new web communication opportunities such as blogging and social-cultural networking sites, have provided independent authors with a new array of modalities to connect with and to expand a growing community of readers, and in the process to create alternative channels to publish and market and tag new work, work that may mix written and audio and visual media but will also continue to be built around books, either paper or digital, as its centerpiece. The writers who take advantage of this opportunity will, in most cases, be those who are adaptive, a bit entrepreneurial, early adopters on, at least, the production side of the creative equation. Those of us who adopt this approach will, along with likeminded readers, be in the best position to regain the upper hand and turn the tables on the huge corporate publishing empires – the literary-industrial complex, if you will – that have ceased to serve us well.

To come at things in a slightly different way, these cataclysmic changes have brought us to a sentinel moment in the history of the publishing industry, a moment from which it is now not only possible, but rather easy, to imagine the world of publishing without publishing companies (in their traditional, recognizable form, at least).

In this new world, with apologies to Irina Dunn, an author needs a publishing company like a fish needs a bicycle.

Digital technology is changing everything, especially everything associated with the arts and with information. If you are an author, you can be as old-school and anti-technology as you like, but it is time to pay attention, because these changes are fundamentally restructuring the relationships between writers and the publishing world, between writers and the world of bookselling and marketing, and most importantly between writers and readers. As a writer, you are now in a position to focus directly on how you want your writing world to work, on a daily basis and over the course of your entire career, and to take direct control over the steps that can make it a reality.

Never underestimate the importance, for you as an author, of what the corporate marketing types call a "brand relationship." There are millions of people on this planet who believe they have a book to write, but they have never thought about having a brand relationship with readers, booksellers, or reviewers. But Stephen King has a brand, and so do Sue Miller and Toni Morrison and Dave Eggers and Charles Bukowski. James Frey had a brand, then he got another one, and to his credit he is now developing a third that represents an honest incorporation of each of the first two woven into the new one. Walt Whitman and Sarah Vowell and Malcolm X have brands, and you can have one too. It isn't something you can buy, and it isn't the name of a publisher on the spine of your book. Your brand will be based on what you write, on the life you have lived (or not), on how you build your relationship with your readers, and on how you present yourself to them through your web presence.

If you can build a following of a thousand readers, and care for and nurture that following one reader at a time, one email at a time, one post at a time, one story or book at a time, it can become the key – along with all your hard work – to your future success as a professional author. Your following, your readers – they are the people who will look forward to the publication of your next book. Not only will they read it, but they will tell others about it and buy copies for them as gifts. They will write customer reviews about it. If they hear you have an article or interview somewhere they will find it. If they hear that you are giving a reading they will come and sit in the front row and ask better-than-average questions. Sometimes they will even populate your imagination as your putative audience. Never fail to thank them for their kindnesses, or they may decide you are a prima donna and turn on you just as quickly as they adopted you. Some of them will be other writers; keep *them* especially close because better than any other readers they know what you need to succeed and they understand the price you have paid to earn the respect that they have for your work. The best audience in the world is composed of other writers who are not weighed down by petty jealousies.

It won't happen overnight. Building reader relationships is not just a matter of selling books. It is engagement. Your communications, notes, and narratives on your blog or website can give real texture and meaning to your relationships with readers.

As an author, it may not have occurred to you that you are looking for a relationship with readers, or that it would be apt to label the desired relationship a "brand relationship." But that is exactly what most of us want as authors, because it is crucial both to our future abilities to sell our books and other writing, to feel connected with readers, to understand in an honest and unfiltered way who is our audience, and to have a sense of control, and even of privacy, over our future as writers.

(If you feel a little crowded or commoditized by my application of the word "brand" to these relationships, I won't push it. I invite you to select your own terminology, and to drop mine, perhaps after you've finished reading this book. I use the word primarily because it has important operational implications).

A blog or website can be extremely helpful in building an audience of readers who feel that they know something about us, who follow us as writers, who bookmark it and make a mental note of it and feel a connection to us when they learn that we have something new out, or something to say about the events of the day whether these are events in literature or in the world at large or in our specific field of expertise or some combination thereof.

A blog allows us to keep and to build upon our community of readers, to keep track of them, and to offer them various forms of reciprocity wherein they can keep track of us.

At any given time each of us has hundreds, or perhaps thousands, of books on the bookshelves of our home or the offices or rooms where we work. Possession of these books is, for bibliophiles, a wonderful thing, but it does not mean that we have "relationships" with all of the authors of these books: there are limits to our promiscuity. There might be one or a dozen or at the outside perhaps a hundred such real relationships, and whenever they exist we tend to cherish them. We may even wish there were more connection available to us as the readers who appreciate these writers' gifts the most.

Over the course of a writer's life she makes and builds upon a promise about who she is, about her integrity and authenticity, and in every future interaction with her readers she must remain true to that promise or carefully reshape it with an equally authentic change in the arc of her narrative, her career, her life. There can be radical changes and forced re-navigations or retreats, as long as a serious writer maintains her authenticity.

Some writers are total chameleons, and they have every right to be. The more you build connection with a community of readers, the more you may be setting yourself up for a hard fall if they sense that you take an implausible detour or become something beyond their understanding of your brand, like all the pissed off fans when Dylan went electric. Although Dylan did not have a blog, eventually he educated his audience to expect change.

Do not oversell your authenticity, integrity, honesty, engagement, mutual trust, or passion for a particular topic if to do so would hem in your creativity as a writer. You have every right to re-invent yourself, if you wish to do so, with every new book that you write. If that is the likely direction of your writing career you may even want to present yourself that way from the get-go.

Meaning, in our connection with readers, comes not from products or prices or book sales but from what we share about how we work, the sound of our readings, shared experiences, how we see the world and our work and other writers. These connections are not necessarily all warm and fuzzy, but they are engaged. These are the relationships that lead most often to word of mouth, buzz, exponential expansion of readership, and viral extension of your audience connections.

If your blog is going to be the common terrain of your relationship-building activities with readers, make it permanent. Think it through existentially so that you are prepared to talk or write about its importance to you as a writer. Do not miss any opportunity to direct readers to it. Consider making your blog's URL address and the name of your "publishing company" *the same* so that, for instance, every Amazon detail page and the spine of every book you sell directs readers to your blog.

When creative people fail in their marketing efforts, it often occurs not because they failed to make the most of the opportunities that they *recognized* as marketing opportunities, but because of other situations for which they failed to realize that a marketing opportunity was at hand. Every page or page element where your work is referenced, whether it is on the Amazon site, your AmazonConnect blog, your own blog or website, elsewhere on the web, or in the physical world, should be inter-linked and connected into a continuous loop that builds awareness of, and markets, your work. Making these connections is not spamming nor scamming, as long as, in any forum, you abide by the culture and etiquette of the community in which you are participating.

Maintain balance. The more time, energy, creativity, and care you devote to your web presence, the more you must also demand in terms of the quality of your primary work as a writer, the work you do in your books, articles, and other writing. Expect and try to build upon the potential for cross-fertilization between this other writing and the writing you may do, for instance, for a blog, particularly if you are writing non-fiction, writing about information and knowledge.

Unless you are J.D. Salinger, building your base of readers requires that you continue to add meaningful depth and content to the bond that initially connected you with readers. Naturally, the most obvious way for you to achieve this is with subsequent publications, but such publication need not be limited to books. (If you are J.D. Salinger, thank you for reading my book. I would be happy to provide a blurb for your next book if you will write one for mine.)

Don't make the mistake of seeing the work that you do to build your web presence as formulaic or elementary. Alongside your actual writing, this work is the central work of your writing life, career, and readership, and it should reflect daily imaginative thought and meditation.

Allowing readers to connect with you through a website invites them to relate not only to the stories you write but to *your story* as an author. In that invitation there may be an implicit level of transparency that pushes beyond your comfort level, so think this through from the get-go. Many of us, for myriad reasons good, bad, and unclassifiable, tend to compartmentalize our lives: between public and private, between process and product, and perhaps between our primary and ancillary narratives. It is a good idea to understand as much as you can about this play of light and shadow in your life, in any case, but that is all the more important if you are imagining any sort of online presence for yourself.

An author's professional blog or website may be your first small step along the artistic pathway of taking control over the means of production of your creative work. In most other artistic fields -- music and recording, film, "radio" broadcast, dance, the stage, painting and photography, even television -- there are important, relatively recent "indie" movements through which artists and creative talent (sometimes locally, and sometimes across entire cultures and continents) have challenged the hegemony of the artistic establishment, or perhaps more precisely, the artistic production establishment. Where books are concerned, there is a rich history of terrific writers self-publishing or organizing what were essentially "micro-publishers" such as Lawrence Ferlinghetti's City Lights Books, but there is also a nasty stigma attached to such efforts whenever they can be dismissed as the vanity work of delusional, talent-free, self-serving writers promoting themselves.

Sometimes, of course, that is exactly what they are. Any of us who would consider promoting or supporting a movement of authors taking the initiative for getting good work more directly into the hands of discerning readers must guard against the mistake of campaigning so simplistically for artistic "democracy" that he may be construed as standing in opposition to excellence and quality, just as the independent authors and publishers who put themselves and their various forms of capital at stake in such a movement must be rigorous in ensuring that the publications in which they invest are of a quality that significant numbers of readers will deem worthy of their time and investment. And for these purposes, blogs and digital publications can be appropriate ways to test the waters.

*   *   *

Why we write need never change. How we write may evolve, but it will always be driven by our nature, our inner architecture as humans. But how we connect our writing with readers is constantly subject to change, and we have arrived now in a potentially revolutionary time when the confluence of technological change and cultural and social change could transform the economics and the reach of writing and reading. The nature of this time makes it desirable, perhaps even imperative, for authors to become students of these changes.

This nexus of change extends far beyond the technology of blogs, or even of the internet as a whole. During the last two decades -- roughly since the mid-1980s -- technological advances such as digitalized short-run printing, desktop publishing and page design, the birth of online bookselling channels, and recent revolutionary developments in e-books and print on demand have created relatively inexpensive and sometimes free opportunities for independent authors and publishers to bring their books to market and get them into the hands of readers. In spite of the stigma associated with self-publishing and vanity presses and considerable resistance on the part of many of the gatekeepers of the traditional publishing industry -- including the publishers themselves, book review media literary agents, and some booksellers, wholesalers, and distributors -- the indie publishing movement has grown explosively from a blip on the radar to well over 50,000 entrepreneurial small publishers today, including a growing number of little presses formed around writers' communities that are direct descendants of earlier ventures such as Lawrence Ferlinghetti's City Lights Press, organized among the Beat writers of the 1950s from the base of his City Lights Bookstore in San Francisco.

Today it is a movement, quite possibly, in which writers and readers may regain the upper hand and turn the tables on huge corporate publishers -- the literary-industrial complex, if you will -- who have ceased to serve them well. Its readers include (but are certainly not limited to) many of the same people who have provided audience for similar "indie music" and "indie film" movements that blossomed in the second half of the 20th century.

If we get too bogged down in the "feel" of creative work or in desultory and marginal definitions of what constitutes "independent" creative work, we run the risk of missing or squandering the greatest opportunities for change. To return to the figure of the fish and the bicycle, what is most powerful about the revolutionary developments in the forms of production that are available to authors today is that they will force change in the economic and cultural relationships that have governed the publishing industry for too long. Neither traditional publishers nor traditional booksellers are necessary when writers and readers are able to connect directly with one another.

There is also an inspiring felicity in the overwhelming logic with which many of these same changes in technology -- that have allowed independent author-publishers to use effective, affordable new processes for producing and marketing their literary work -- also empower readers and other newly minted literary gatekeepers to share the buzz and communication that helps to identify and spread the news about what is worth reading and to get it into the hands of willing readers. This viral process goes beyond branding; it is life in a literary tribe. It resists top-down corporate branding and it resists pressure to commoditize or to replicate in any cheap or formulaic way what seems in one case to have appeal. It relies upon authenticity and the willingness of readers and writers to find new and intimate ways to identify with and engage each other.

Chapter III.4

The Meaning and Value
Of an Author's Presence on the Web

Let's start by staking out a very straightforward and modest umbrella phrase -- "online culture" -- to describe a range of different kinds of communication and community including the blogosphere, user groups, cultural websites, e-zines, chat rooms, bulletin boards, open information resources, online social networks, and interactive websites operated by everyone from individuals to labor unions to social change organizations to news organizations to political campaigns to commercial sites such as Ebay and Amazon.com. Taken together, this online culture is no longer just a reflection of the formerly larger physical-world culture; now it *is* the culture. Among many other things it is a seemingly transparent and sometimes democratic platform for communication and testimony about artistic and creative work, and it is also the canvas for much of that art, whether visual or musical or textual.

Online culture facilitates branding and filtering distinctions among its subcultures and communities, and these distinctions can be every bit as powerful as the distinctions that more monolithic corporate media attempt to broadcast in forms, for examples, such as television commercials and billboard ads. Within these subcultures and communities there are myriad different approaches to the customs, ethics, and etiquette of marketing and communication behavior (i.e., what constitutes self-promotion, or shilling, or spam?) and the debate about these different approaches can often become so intense and white-hot among purists and partisans that it threatens to take over or even wipe out the underlying communities.

One fascinating characteristic of much of this online culture exists in the fact that many of its websites and blogs allow a seamless equivalence between content and traffic. Various technologies from website or blog traffic to Amazon Sales Rankings to Google searches provide means of measuring traffic and buzz and sales almost simultaneously, and in the process they multiply and enhance the existing trends in the behavior of each community's population, customers, or readers. If you search for information sources on a particular topic in the online culture you can expect to find that the most trafficked (or linked) sources will come up at the head of the resulting search list. You will also be able easily to find substantial excerpts from several of the sources, and customer-feedback information that may assist you in determining whether to purchase material from a given vendor. All of this information is, in one sense or another, branding information, and while it can be subjected to manipulation, there is useful general transparency. More often than not the truth will out.

If this new world of the written world appeals to you, keep your eyes open. There is no point in entering this world unless you are prepared to set your mind to unknown arts, and to focus some of your energies in an entrepreneurial way on the processes of marketing and promoting your work, and yourself as an author.

If you've come this far, it should come as no surprise that the natural locus for these efforts will be the web, and the natural hub that will serve as the organizing center of these efforts should be your personal author's website. (This will be true, of course, regardless of whether or not you intend to maintain ties with traditional publishers).

Fortunately, many of the activities involved in taking advantage of these opportunities do not involve daunting technical hurdles.

Although keeping a blog is often described by journalists as "keeping an online journal," it is actually much more than that. However informal and conversational much blog writing may be in style, and in spite of the fact that the medium is understandably associated, quite often, either with politics or with the personal confessionals of self-absorbed, exhibitionistic 23-year-olds drawn compulsively to discuss their adventures in sex, rock, and video, the other reality is increasingly that blogs provide a professional platform of information and expression in every field of intellectual, technical, recreational, consumer, and creative interest. They will soon be read by more people than any other single medium, and the velocity of their growth is stunning.

Like independent book publishing itself, or like indie filmmaking or indie music, blogging is both a way to circumvent traditional media and a way to attract and co-opt traditional media. Whenever alternative channels such as blogs begin to thrive, one of the most predictable responses among the hipper elements of corresponding traditional media is to surf those new technologies scouting for edgy new talent. Just as movie moguls are known to swoop down on the creative talent at Sundance and South by Southwest with their checkbooks at the ready, the writers' and publishers' trade magazines can't get enough of stories about bloggers with book contracts. After all, for a young literary agent or editor who wants to put her own "I discovered a gem" stamp on the material she is bringing to her next meeting, an interesting blogger may have the perfect combination of observable writing skills, pre-existing market identity, credibility as an expert, platform for future promotion, and the panache or branding potential of a new-media pedigree.

Indie culture is constantly available to the mainstream or corporate culture, even if it isn't always noticed. Although a frequent concomitant of such scoutings and signings may be the purist's charge that "so and so is a sell-out," these cultural cross-overs are generally beneficial to all concerned: they build credibility for the blog or other indie platform in question with artists or audience alike, they tend to bring much-needed creative diversity and edginess to the mainstream and thus to extend the brand or the company or imprint involved, and, at least in the short run, they provide the "new" talent with a paycheck.

Our polemical energies aside, there is little percentage for any creative artist in going through one's creative career as a rigid purist; the definitions, alliances, and audiences are all too protean to reward a commitment beyond one's own aesthetics, belief system, and self-preservation instincts. What is important is that every writer bring an intense mindfulness to her relationships with her audience and with those who might play the role of gatekeeper between artist and audience. There is much to be said for an author signing a contract that allows her to thrive by leaving to specialists the work of production, editing, design, and marketing, particularly if the contract is a fine arrangement that grants very specific rights and holds the other party accountable for very specific responsibilities.

But lest we get too far ahead of ourselves here, let's focus on the considerable benefits that blogging holds for the independent author-publisher:

· The discipline of daily writing in your area(s) of interest and expertise, which is a must if you are to maintain currency and audience interest in your blog, will develop and test the two most important prerequisites for someone who wants to succeed in writing a book on a given subject, the quality of your writing and your passion for the subject matter.

· A blog can provide you with a platform and an audience, depending of course on the quality, currency, and interest of what you have to say. When one considers the fact that a sell-through of 3,000 to 5,000 copies total can spell modest success either for an independently published book or for a debut narrative work published by a small press or literary imprint, it is easy to understand why having even a relatively small blog following of 200 to 300 regular readers can be enormously beneficial to the early success of a book you are bringing out. Buzz breeds buzz, sales breeds sales, and the book sales you can generate through your blog audience may vault you to a more favorable early Amazon sales ranking, which could provide you with better placement throughout the Amazon website. A discounted pre-publication sales offer that sells several dozen copies to your blog following could even help to defray any upfront costs for your book.

· The interactive process of blog-posting and the connectedness with the world of information that is likely to go hand-in-hand with your blogging activities can provide you with a rather intense content feedback system in your areas of expertise. If you write about culture or technology or business, or even if you write fiction or narrative nonfiction, you may find that early draft versions of the material that lands ultimately in your next book come frequently out of your daily blogosphere discourse.

· As your independent publishing project achieves success, it will also help to build your stature as a blogger, and your blogging platforms will continue to be a powerful and extremely inexpensive way to communicate with existing and potential audience.

*   *   *

There is a now rather famous old cartoon from the *New Yorker* that inspired such familiar pleasure for me when I first saw it that I have assumed, perhaps unfairly, that it is, itself, derivative: two dogs sit in front of a computer terminal, one observing as the other types away at what we may presume are email or chat-room communications and says, aside, "On the internet, nobody knows you're a dog."

The importance of the phenomenon that this cartoon illustrates is not so much that our online culture hides us from view or allows a bit of privacy as that, in the process, it invites tens of millions of individuals among us, in some way or other, to invent ourselves anew. And while our mass culture may predictably focus on the banality of, say, entire chat rooms whose only participants are middle-aged men posing as twenty-something lesbians and bi-curious seventeen-year-old schoolgirls, I am far more interested in the more subtle alchemy of people who seek, online and elsewhere, to mine and illuminate something previously unexpressed or unrecognized in themselves. Sometimes these efforts are purely delusional or strictly recreational, as with the millions of guys who spend hours playing online at being the general managers of fantasy baseball teams that compete for points, prizes, or self-esteem by drafting, trading, and demoting athletes who "in real life" earn millions by posting the statistics from which the meta-currency of the online games is distilled. As one who has been there and done that, I can attest that such a parallel universe can be quite seductive, because it offers not only the underlying alternate reality but also millions of choices for alternatives selves, for us to slip into alternative skins in which we may be far more comfortable than in our own, and in which we can thrill to so many little false exhilarations that we may be able to attain a state of sufficient confusion as to convince ourselves that, at least for a few hours, we don't lead lives of quiet desperation.

But without wishing to cast any aspersions on such vehicles for doing the time of our existence, I focus instead on the millions of us for whom online culture offers opportunities to create, to experience and appreciate, to comment upon, to expand upon or sample or riff off or counter, works of ideas or art or imagination or history. In the mid-1990s it may have seemed to many observers that the early adopters who engaged in these activities online were only reflecting in some skewed way the culture of the much more significant "real world," but the truth now in the early 21st century is that, while cybersex may not be real sex, online creative culture is as much the real deal as you are likely to get from any deck of "real-world" cards. To acknowledge this is not a testament to how hip or "wired" one is, but a simple nod to the present realities of cultural commerce, comment, and creation. Music, film, photography, and text are regularly created, read, shared, viewed, bought and sold, stolen, or buzzed about online in roughly the same proportions as occur in the physical world. For artistic efforts that can be transmitted or shared online without loss of dimension, in complexity or impact, the internet, even though it may lack the gritty and compelling authenticity proofs of a converted factory or warehouse site in DUMBO, is the ultimate "alternative space."

These developments offer us, as individuals, a kind of cover, not anonymity or the ability to achieve transgender or post-canine transubstantiation so much as an untethering from our quotidian realities and the ways, physical, economic, and otherwise, in which we are seen, sorted, and stigmatized by others every day. Through this untethering many of us experience a great unleashing of our individual creativity, as in many cases we begin to transcend the self-filtering, self-censoring processes that are hardwired into us in the course of our formative interactions with our economic environments and educational systems. In turns, of course, lest there be concern that distinctions of quality will go begging, we submit and subject ourselves to the far more intense and instantaneous feedback that is supported and enabled in the online culture whenever we express ourselves, which is probably more effective as an intervention against self-delusion or mediocrity in art or ideas than dismissal by traditional hierarchies, precisely because it is more authentic, real-time, transparent and, in the composition of its putative jury, more democratic, than any judgment offered by editors, agents, reviewers, or teachers.

Equally important, participation in the online culture increasingly offers the potential for immediate synthesis of several kinds of feedback that are important in varying degrees to most creative people: traffic, comment, and compensation. On the literary internet, from Amazon.com to book blogs to the websites of authors and libraries and publishers, readers are writers and writers are readers. Comment is a legitimate form of content, and traffic (whether it is measured in hits or readers or units sold) is both comment and content.

In this potential Eden of unfettered imagination, viral intellect, and global audience, the greatest sin, the sin whose penalty is banishment from the garden, is not sin itself but a lack of authenticity. Advertising is dead, online culture is inherently anti-corporate, and while we may give huge companies a pass if they spell their corporate names with lower-case letters, there is easy consensus that to spam and to shill and to self-promote are the worst forms of self-tarnishing behavior.

The best commercial websites tend to be very effective not only at appealing to the community-seeking instinct in many of us, but at actively engaging that instinct by providing opportunities to share perspectives, to link to one's existing communities or to augment them by finding others with similar interests, and to explore and even create networks of early adopters and peer "buzz agents" and avid camp followers who provide a natural -- but also commercially effective -- collaborative filtering process in ways that advance the market viability of some products over others, and specifically for our purposes some books or music or films over others. The aptest employees and managers of these retail sites -- those whom Meg Whitman or Jeff Bezos, respectively, might say understand best what it means to be "ebaysian" or "amazonian" -- maintain a delicate balance wherein they build community without every explicitly commoditizing community, even while they may be aware that for millions of their customers the chance to express themselves about, say, the latest Sue Miller novel may be every bit as much of a draw as "free shipping for orders over $25."

Visitors to sites like Amazon and Ebay often find their experiences so "sticky" that they stay for extended periods, return again and again, and experience a total blurring of any demarcations as to whether they are there as consumers, members, readers, entrepreneurs, critics, sellers, gossips, browsers, researchers, industry observers, music clip addicts, or internet zombies. Personally, I have found that Amazon is often the best place to recover the lost address and telephone number of a friend, colleague, or relative if I have ever had occasion to send that person a gift book, album, or other gift. Jeff Bezos and his company will always have their ardent detractors (for many of whom, one suspects, the aforementioned activities may be guilty secret pleasures); after all, Bezos has become a billionaire (nine times over) after starting the confounded outfit in his garage, and their are plenty of worthy bookpeople who blame Amazon, in any given week, for the demise of independent bookstores, author royalties, or the grand old New York publishers. But for most of us who inhabit most intensely the world of readers, writers, bibliophiles and sojourners in the book trade, Amazon is a seductive and extremely informative place where one can read, browse, compare the sales records of our favorite or fellow authors, discover what other individuals or entire communities or companies are reading, or scout for promising new content for rights deals. In a very real sense, for many of us who physically go to work each day at our writing desks or in publishers' offices or in libraries or bookstores or university writing and literature programs or countless other outposts of our literary culture, we also go to work each day at Amazon and elsewhere on the literary internet.

It should come as no surprise, then, that this same literary internet provides authors and publishers with unprecedented opportunities to engage real readers and book buyers with our literary or textual output, provided that we honor cultural etiquette by maintaining the delicate balance, previously referenced, between building community and commoditizing it, or between expressing ourselves as authors and cultural citizens, and, well, hawking our wares. The late Paris Review fountainhead George Plympton is said to have commented that the entire subscription list upon which that venerable journal could depend from year to year was comprised of literary MFA program matriculants, libraries, and a small group of seriously literary authors. Are a sufficient proportion of this literary redeeming remnant sufficiently conversant with the ways of the internet that one might hope to reach them by marketing to them over the Internet? Yes, they are, and indeed if they were not, it would probably be our responsibility to help bring them along. Whatever else one thinks of its vast online marketplace, one can't help but conclude that Amazon has done more than anyone or anything else to train readers and writers in the ways of the Internet.

*   *   *

Throughout this book I may have occasionally have conveyed the inaccurate impression that "blog" and "website" are interchangeable terms for the same thing. They are not. The confusion comes mainly from that fact that I am strongly advocating that authors make use of the incredibly user-friendly, inexpensive tools, services, architecture, and hosted domains of blogging services to create full-featured authors' websites without having to learn how to speak, translate, and read HTML, XML, or any other distinctly foreign language.

In other words, it is not my intention to recommend that an author's website should be primarily an "online journal" or "linked commentary," although these are the two kinds of websites associated most frequently with blogging. There's nothing wrong with either of these forms of expression, and you may well make use of them as specific features within the larger geography of your website. But a hosted blogger's platform such as Blogger allows you to build a much more full-featured website with an extremely short learning curve, no experience with code, and no expenditure of funds.

To provide a sense of the kind of features you might wish to include on such a website, here is a menu of possibilities:

· Links to allow readers to buy your work on Amazon or other websites, and to the editorial material that accompanies those detail pages;

· Signed copies for sale directly on your website with PayPal functionality;

· Links to free excerpts from these titles to whet readers appetites;

· Links to the text of your previously published articles, stories, reviews, books, etc., either on your own website or on websites where they originally appeared;

· Your biographical material, in whatever detail you present it, along with links to related material;

· Q & A sessions you wish to make available as text or podcast;

· A place to write and manage the development of any number of works in progress with whatever levels of security and privacy one chooses;

· A place to manage research, information, and knowledge either privately or collaboratively, with whatever levels of security and privacy one chooses;

· A place to build a community of one's readers, with information on readings, signings, speaking engagements, and appearances;

· A workshopping hub for any community of writers, or readers and writers, in which you may be a participant, with whatever levels of security and privacy one chooses;

· Podcasts of you reading your own work, others' work, or any of the above material;

· Graphic images, portfolios of photos, cover designs, illustrations, or other materials associated with your writing;

· Google Earth shots or maps associated with your writing, your bio, or events in which your readers may be interested;

· Your reading recommendations and reviews;

· Permissions and copyright information associated with your writing;

· Materials for agents, editors, reviewers, journalists, and publishers who might wish to contact you;

· Links to features such as Author Tracker, Amazon Connect, Amazon Shorts, or Virtual Book Tours;

· A Submission Tracker for your own use;

· Reviews and reader commentaries on your writing;

· Readers' guides or discussion group guides to your work, as well as other material for booksellers, readers, and others;

· A hub for correspondence, archiving, public domain material, disclaimers, end matter, and rights information; and

· Updates or supplemental material not available at the time a book or other piece of writing was published.

The possibilities are limited only by your own imagination and output. For many of the individuals who are "blogging" throughout the world today, blogs are the main place where they write, and that's fine. Indeed, for many, blogging is to the world of mainstream, traditional journalism as the indie publishing movement and its myriad opportunities (including, of course, blogging) is to traditional, mainstream book publishing. But our focus here is on the role that blogging can play in the work of those of us whose primary purpose is to write books and to get them into the hands of readers.

Blogger's blog hosting structure allows for very tidy, easy-to-navigate mapping of an extremely detailed, dynamic, complex, and protean umbrella web site: a mirror of your professional writing career that grows and changes as you do.

The first law of self-promotion is do not promote yourself, at least not too obviously or nakedly. My point here is not that you should be sneaky about it. Instead, build an interesting and engaging website that presents your material as fully and richly as possible, with as few as possible self-aggrandizing statements of your own, either direct or parenthetical. Provide a structure in which readers can offer feedback, whether of a positive nature or otherwise, and make it easy and attractive for readers and other writers and bloggers and literary gatekeepers to link to you. Consider participating in a multi-blog community of authors. When there is comment about your work elsewhere on the internet, excerpt it honestly and link to it. Let your work and the appeal of your website and the feedback you receive filter and direct people to your writing. This will not make you an overnight wonder, but it will help to organize and gather momentum for your steady growth as an author with an audience, a following, a connected community of readers. Do not be so hungry for hits or eyeballs that you piss people off by spamming them. These things take time. Be true to your work and honor it, and the readers who already appreciate it, with your humility and modesty.

As you maintain your inquisitiveness and do the work necessary to stay abreast of all that is new and changing in the world of the written word, you may sometimes feel inundated with dozens of opportunities and channels for reaching out to potential audience or literary gatekeepers: blogs, podcasts, Author Tracker, Amazon Shorts, virtual book tours, etc., ad infinitum. Let your website be the organizing hub for such activity. Don't stress about it. Just build the appropriate functionalities into your website's menu of features.

Don't kid yourself into thinking that you are so talented, spontaneous, and fluid that you should compose directly into your blog. Compose first in your word-processing program, then edit, fact-check, and spell-check. If your timetable can accommodate it, you might even consider sleeping on your posts before you hit the final "send" button. Every word you post on the internet is permanent, and your professional writing career.... Well, you get it, right?

AFTERWORD

A Back Door to the Publishing Industry

As you may have noticed, one of the benefits that I have proclaimed, for this book specifically and for author websites in general, is that a independent publishing, good marketing, and a serviceable website may provide a writer with a "backchannel" to the world of publishing.

It is a terribly difficult thing to enter the traditional mainstream publishing industry through the front door.

But there are other channels available to you. Writers want readers. Readers yearn to get their hands on good writing. In the middle, brokering the relations between writers and readers, lies a publishing industry whose corporate preoccupations have increasingly distracted it from serving the mutual interest of writers and readers.

Respect your own time as an author. Even if you have been working at minimum wage, you have spent thousands of dollars worth of your time writing the book that you are about to publish. While it is important not to waste your money in the process of publishing and marketing your book, it is bound to be worth some wisely chosen expenditure to give your book the chance to get into the hands of receptive readers.

So, what's wrong with the front door, you ask?

Thank you for asking.

Let's take a step back and look objectively at the world of book publishing today, just a few decades on from the golden age of America's venerable publishing houses: it is not a pretty picture.

The major "American" book publishers that are left standing early in the 21st Century are dominated by five publishing empires, most of them headquartered outside the United States, that produce over three-fourths of all books published in English in the United States. All of these publishers are under enormous structural pressures that make it nearly impossible for them to serve the interests either of readers or of authors, Indeed, while their branding strategies may occasionally pay lip service to such strategies, the hard realities of the boardroom are that, like nearly any other corporation, they are in business to serve their stakeholders. It would be naive to expect otherwise.

The frenzy of global corporate merger and acquisition that swallowed up the stately old publishing houses in the waning decades of the 20th Century has placed a critical mass of "American" publishing power in the hands of a few huge, distinctly global, and singularly profit-driven media and industrial conglomerates like Bertelsmann, Time Warner, and the Rupert Murdoch empire. The old notions that these companies ought to serve some higher cultural purpose is lost for all but a few noble editors like Farrar Straus Giroux' Jonathan Galassi, whose own literary roots, principles, and vision render them almost anachronistic throwbacks to the glorious past of Scribners' Maxwell Perkins and Random House's Jason Epstein.

But hey, what's wrong with a publishing company's need to generate a healthy profit?

Nothing at all.

It is working pretty well for the mega-publishers' stakeholders and it is keeping the wolf from the door of hard-working authors who slave away in their garrets each day, men and women like Paris Hilton, Jimmy Buffett, Bill O'Reilly, Madonna, Jon Stewart, Sean Hannity, Ann Coulter, Danielle Steel, Celine Dion, Tatum O'Neal. Amber Frey, the Swift Boat Veterans, and whatever writers are exercising the license for Tom Clancy's Op center these days.

For the rest of us, we better have a backchannel, because the chances are less than one in a thousand that we can even get a reading from a mainstream publishing house by sending them an unsolicited manuscript. The perverse reality of the publishing industry today is that these celebrity authors are forcing other writers -- serious writers of quality work -- off the bookshelves of our bookstores and libraries, out of any chance of being noted in the major print and electronic book review media, and consequently, in many cases, out of the writing business.

The nature of vertical corporate accountability to ultimate shareholders and stakeholders unfortunately strips away a global company's ground-level ability to pursue any mission so nuanced or complex that it cannot be summed up in a two-minute PowerPoint presentation of quantifiable metrics and scalable revenue benchmarks at the next quarterly planning session. The need to hit the numbers (or be shut down) can drive even the most well-intentioned publishers to focus most or all of their corporate energies on big books by brand-name celebrity authors.

Ride 'em hard, put 'em away wet, and saddle 'em up again tomorrow.

Again and again, the same handful of authors will get their six-figure print runs, seven-figure advances, and the lion's share of their publishers' marketing and promotion budgets, editorial and design attention, and deal-making energy when it comes to things like foreign and subsidiary rights.

But resourceful writers have more options available to them that may at first be apparent. By building a following of readers, and establishing an independent platform, an author may render herself a sought-after commodity among publishers, to the point where she is discovered when her blog demonstrates clearly her writing talent and her authority. As the indie publishing movement gains strength and favor among readers, one of the telling signals of its success occurs when the more tuned-in representatives of the mainstream publishers begin to troll writers' blogs and independent publishers' offerings to scout for fresh new talent that bears an edgy, indie imprimatur.

At that point, when the author's blog demonstrates her expertise, her talent, and her community of readers, she does not need the mainstream publishing industry. She is in a good position to go independent, to publish and market and profit from her book, either solo or with a small group of kindred spirits, and to continue to use her blog to extend her reach as a professional author. The independent path will provide her much greater creative and professional control, and it may even provide her better compensation than she might net from a traditional book contract.

BIBLIOGRAPHY AND RESOURCES

I've spent much of the past decade reading hundreds of books and essays that are relevant to the concerns of this book, but given our growing powers to search out content with the powerful engines of Googlezon, I have come to subscribe to the view that, where bibliographies are concerned, less is more. I consider these books and web resources to be the essentials with respect to the preoccupations that inspired this writing project on my part.

BOOKS AND ARTICLES

Anderson, Chris. The Long Tail: Why the Future of Business is Selling Less of More. Hyperion. 2006.

Epstein, Jason. Book Business: Publishing Past Present and Future. W.W. Norton. 2001.

Kremer, John. 1001 Ways to Market Your Book, 6th Edition. Open Horizons. 2006.

Lessig, Lawrence. The Future of Ideas: The Fate of the Commons in a Connected World. Vintage. 2002.

Poynter, Dan. Dan Poynter's Self Publishing Manual, 16th Edition: How to Write, Print, and Sell Your Own Book. Para Publishing. 2007.

WEB RESOURCES

Institute for the Future of the Book.

Poynter, Dan. Book Industry Statistics. http://bookstatistics.com and ParaPublishing.com

Wikert, Joe. Publishing2020.

Windwalker, Stephen. IndieKindle and A Kindle Home Page.

INDEX

Because of the search power that is automatic with the Kindle, the index for this edition does not include links or page numbers. If you use the search from within the Kindle edition of this document, and type in any word from this index, your Kindle screen will be populated with occurrences of the search term from within this book, elsewhere on your Kindle, and on the web.

www.ingramcontent.com/pod-product-compliance
Lightning Source LLC
LaVergne TN
LVHW011228080426
835509LV00005B/382